Mark Frederick Bigney

The Forest Pilgrims

And Other Poems

Mark Frederick Bigney

The Forest Pilgrims
And Other Poems

ISBN/EAN: 9783744652889

Printed in Europe, USA, Canada, Australia, Japan

Cover: Foto ©Thomas Meinert / pixelio.de

More available books at **www.hansebooks.com**

THE

FOREST PILGRIMS,

AND

OTHER POEMS.

BY

M. F. BIGNEY.

NEW ORLEANS:

JAMES A. GRESHAM,

92 CAMP STREET.

NEW YORK: M. DOOLADY.

1867.

JOHN J. REED, PRINTER AND STEREOTYPER,

43 Centre Street, N. Y.

THIS

LITTLE VOLUME,

PRODUCED IN "HOURS OF IDLENESS,"

IS

RESPECTFULLY AND AFFECTIONATELY DEDICATED

TO

FRIENDS AND RELATIVES,

WIDELY SCATTERED OVER A "BOUNDLESS CONTINENT."

New Orleans, December, 1866.

CONTENTS.

x CONTENTS.

THE FOREST PILGRIMS.

[There is a tradition to the effect that one of the original
Pilgrim Fathers, after sojourning for some years in the Old
Colony, became dissatisfied with the treatment he had
received at the hands of his brethren, and with his two
children, a son and daughter, abandoned civilization, crossed
the Alleghany mountains, and both he and his were slain by
the Indians.]

A LONELY cottage in New England stood,
    Where a fair glade in the majestic wood
Opened its hill-side bosom to the breeze,
Whose wings had wanton'd o'er Atlantic seas.
Beside a casement in that cottage were
A brother and a sister, fond and fair :
Suited to each, there was in either face,
A well-apportioned beauty which might grace
Earth's highest courts ; while round them love
    divine
Threw its effulgence, as a sacred sign.
  'Twas on an eve in May. The rosy sheen
Of evening lingered o'er that sylvan scene,

And the fond promise of a morrow, bright,
Gave added glories to approaching night.
On the fair scene the gazers, ling'ring, look.
The air was balm. The music of a brook
Mingled melodious with the vesper hymn
Of nature's minstrels from each forest limb.
'Twas their last evening gaze. That lovely pair
Would wander with the dawn—they knew not
  where.
Forsaking and forsaken—ask not why
The tear-drop lingered in each youthful eye.
 Their sire approached ; a hale though aged man,
In whose determined visage one might scan
A look of firmness, in which deep intent
And pious resignation both were blent.
A man he was whom force could ne'er subdue ;
Who rendered worship, free and pure and true,
To Freedom, Purity and Truth—to God
Who guides in mercy His avenging rod.
He stood within the cottage of the glade,
O'er which the maple threw its em'rald shade,
And smiled upon his children. He had braved
The storm's loud fury when it madly raved ;
The persecutor's ire ; the vengeful cry
Of the red warrior, when he sought to try
His prowess on the pale-face. To possess
A lodgment in the boundless wilderness,
Where God alone in love and nature smiled—
A sanctuary in the pathless wild—
He had resolved to leave his cottage home

With his two treasures farther still to roam.
"Fair ones," said he, "fond children of my love,
William, Matilda, may the powers above
Direct our counsels and our footsteps guide
When far away we wander side by side.
God be our guiding star, our beacon light,
Our never-failing refuge day and night,
And blessings will attend our weary way,
And be our answers when we humbly pray.
   All things are ready.   With the morning sun
Our westward journey must be well begun.
We seek a home where God's green mountains
      high
Uprear their crests to kiss the bending sky.
I sought this shore, one of the Pilgrim band,
Who fled from persecution's iron hand,
But those who were my brethren mock me now
With that old taunt—' I'm holier than thou !'
O, they forget the trials past ; the toil
Which made this ancient wilderness to smile !
The sacred rights of conscience they arraign ;
The sacred banner of the Cross they stain,
And while from persecution they are free
They learn to persecute both mine and me.
What longer binds us here ? Freedom of thought—
The boon for which this solitude I sought—
No longer here is found.   The vasty deep
Chants ceaseless dirges where the ashes sleep
Of what was once your mother.   Let them swell—
These sad but holy tears !   Yet bid farewell,

Without repining, to these sylvan scenes :
We'll seek another home where evergreens
Hang their fair curtains round some peaceful spot,
And there in freedom will we build our cot."

Wild was the fancy of that fearless man,
Who sought no counsel, but of God, to plan
The way he was to wander.   In his choice
He felt the promptings of " a still small voice,"
Which whispered ever hope and trust and cheer,
And banished from his soul all thoughts of fear.

The parent-pilgrim, ere he slept that night,
And ere he started with the morrow's light
Poured forth his spirit to the Guide above—
The Perfect Counsellor, whose name is Love—
Praying protection from that Master-hand
Which guided Moses to the promised land.

The first faint glimmering of morning sheen,
Contending empire with night's calm serene,
Broke in the east to hail that triune band
Bending their steps as to some promised land.
And on, and on they journeyed, till all trace
Of bigot-bondage and of Europe's race
Was lost in the deep forest's pathless wild ;
But Nature triumphed there, and Freedom smiled,
And faith, with stronger pinion, sought the throne
Of Him who rules the universe alone.

O happy wanderers ! with little blest !
Contentment dwelt with them, a sacred guest.
The forest gave them sustenance and shade
And every eve a tent of boughs was made,

Where, serenaded by the whip-poor-will,
In peace they slept.   The kindled flame was still
Their watchful guardian from the beasts of prey,
Till with their prayers they hailed returning day.
   Thus on they wandered.   Flow'rets everywhere
Adorned their pathway and perfumed the air,
While many a tuneful tenant of the grove
On painted pinions, seemed with them to rove.
The scenes around were fair, and wild, and bright,
As poet's dream, tinged with elysian light,
And all was blended in one blissful prayer
To Him whose glory fills earth, sea and air.
   At length, on Alleghany's crest they stood—
A crest, by echoes haunted, crowned with wood,—
Just as the sun, at close of fairest day,
Gilded that summit with a golden ray.
Matilda here, enamored of the scene,
Gazed on the wide expanse of living green,
As a new revelation, kindly given
By the great Architect of earth and heaven.
She saw beneath her vasty heaps of earth,
Like giant children of chaotic birth,
Nestling in fondness, or reclined at rest,
Around that higher heap's maternal breast.
She loved to think upon their rock-bound base,
Which God alone could fashion or displace :
She loved the flowers which grew beneath the
      trees
And gave their odors to the wooing breeze ;
She loved the birds' soft pean, when they strove

To still the hoarser echoes of the grove ;
She loved the murmur of the mountain rill,
Which all those ancient forest heights did fill
With gushing melody ; while every pine,
Through its high boughs, became a harp divine.

    But from that Pisgah-top her worthy sire
Looked on the Western vallies, to admire
Their wide-spread promise. On and onward still,
Spake the firm voice of his controlling will ;
And on and onward did that band proceed :
All joyously determined ; they agreed
To brave the torrent and the rough descent :
Danger found courage : peace became content.

    Far in the vale advanced, at length they found
A beauteous tract of undulating ground ;
And there, on a savannah of the wood,
The village of a forest-chieftain stood.
They sought the hunters of the wild : their Brave
The welcome of a kingly warrior gave.
He bade them culture friendship's fruitful tree ;
To smoke the calumet of peace : to be
His honored guests, the children of his care,
Welcome as flow'rs of Spring ; as morning, fair.

    The elder pilgrim bowed, and thus replied :—
" Brother and Chief, thou seest by thy side
A man who knows of sorrow, not of fears ;
Whose locks are whit'ning with the frost of years;
Whose strength begins to fail him, and whose
      sight
Is not so piercing as in manhood's might.

I am too old for war.   Time's tide must cease
Ere long for me ; then let it roll in peace,
While I upon the changeful stream am borne
To that fair land which knows of no return—
That happy home—the spirit's hunting-ground—
Where ever-bearing trees of life abound—
That lovely island where the weary rest,
And the Great Spirit smiles upon the blest.
Give me a spot of ground which shall be free ;
I'll rear a lodgment there for mine and me,
And there we'll live.   With corn I'll plant my
    land,
And fondly nurse it with a careful hand,
And when the Spirit of the Harvest sends
Those yellow treasures, which His bounty lends
To those who till the soil, the blest increase
I'll share with thee in thankfulness and peace.
My boy amid your hunters shall be free
To tread the forest, and to climb the tree ;
To speed the arrow in its destined course,
With noble daring and with manly force ;
To scorn the fetters of the crouching slave,
And speak amid the Councils of the Brave.
My girl, the tender flow'ret of my care,
Must live within my cabin, to prepare
My maize and venison ; to watch my fire,
And cheer with songs her brother and her sire.
Your maidens' songs, she too shall learn to sing—
Blithe as the birds which carol in the Spring—
To welcome back the hunter from the chase,

And the young Brave who triumphs in the race.
Chieftain, my words are ended : wilt thou bring
To me the shelter of thy eagle wing,
When storms are sweeping through the clouds
    above ;
And when they pass—the quiet of the dove ?"
  " It shall be as thou wilt "—the Chief resumed ;
And then he called around his warriors plumed,
And, with a graceful movement of his hand,
He said : " Go bound a portion of my land
To be to the pale children of the sun
As tillage ground."   He spoke and it was done.
    Time fleetly passed.   Night's empress waxed
      and waned ;
Still, harmony and sweet contentment reigned
Between the pilgrims and their forest friends,
And every day new proof of friendship lends.
The son and daughter of the forest Chief,
" Young Buffalo" and the fair " Maple-leaf,"
To William and Matilda soon became
As children of one father.   Choicest game
Young Buffalo would to Matilda bring ;
And William unto Maple-leaf would sing
The songs of love, and read the Book of Life,
Whose words divine should calm all earthly strife.
The youthful chieftain was of stalwart frame,
And Maple-leaf, a dusky nymph, whose fame
Had circled far and wide.   How dear, how fair,
The pale-faced strangers to these Indians were !
How wonderful the stories that they told !

How marvellous a speech which they *behold*—
A silent speech which to the eye appears,
And mocks the office of the idle ears !
But stranger still than e'en the written word,
Were the great tidings which thus came, unheard—
A message from the skies.   How fair and bright
Seemed Bethlehem's Star, which made their dark-
  ness light ;
How grand and holy that sublime decree,
Which bade from wrath to come the sinner flee !
Wild superstitions all were cast away,
As an old garment, and eternal day
Beamed on their minds, till their uncultured lays
Were all translated into songs of praise.

 And then in turn the dusky converts told
Their wild traditions from the days of old,
And the strange stories which had filled their ears
Of pale-faced nations who of gods were peers.
How they had come from a far, distant shore ;
How vast canoes these wondrous people bore ;
How in their vengeance, with a potent breath,
They bade the thunder do their work of death ;
How, in their realm, the sun's refulgent crest,
Waves o'er his sea-bed in his hours of rest,
With golden glory which affords delight
To warrior-ghosts that wander in the night ;
How, in vast bubbles, sailing through the sky,
They trace the secrets of the stars on high ;
And how wild beasts, subdued at their command,
Whirl them in chariots o'er the solid land.

At length strange rumors circled far and near,
Pointed and venomed by a dusky seer,
And all the tribe seemed brought to direst grief,
By the apostate children of their Chief.
A council soon was called, when 'twas decreed
That the pale-fac'd deceivers all should bleed.
The seer pronounced their doom :

                    " Accursed be they,
Who would not such ungrateful demons slay !
Accurs'd be all who would not tortures bring—
The poison'd arrow and the serpent's sting—
The burning fagot of the red man's ire,
Which leads to death by slow consuming fire.
Each pale-face is a fiend !   With serpent wile,
He crawls and flatters only to beguile ;
He steals our lands, deceives us to destroy,
And, with fire-water, brings infernal joy,
Which maddens every sense and bows the soul
In misery and shame.   Let thunders roll,
And the Great Spirit flash out from the sky,
Those flaming arrows which speak vengeance nigh!
No home among us for the pale-faced band !
No reptile race to curse our noble land !
The red-man, to be free, must stand alone,
And when the white man comes, the white man's
      groan
Must be the red man's music.   Let the feast
For the wild vulture and the wilder beast,
Be soon prepared.   Before three days are o'er,
Let it be said : ' These reptiles are no more.' "

Soon to the ear of the young Buffalo
Such tidings came as 'whelmed his soul in woe.
He heard the doom pronounced against his friends;
But the high courage which religion lends,
Roused in his soul the will to do and dare ;
To save his friends or their worst dangers share.
　　Night came—a night of storm.　The thunder's
　　　peal
Seemed on the seer's decree to set the seal
Of the Great Spirit.　Oak and stately ash
Were rived to splinters by the angry flash
Of Manitau, the Just ; while the cold rain
Of autumn fell unpitying on the plain.
　　Through storm and darkness, strong in spite of
　　　grief,
Young Buffalo and the fond Maple-leaf,
With stealthy steps the pilgrim's cabin sought,
And cried—" Escape! we too, will share your lot."
　　And hurried preparation soon was made ;
A solemn prayer was uttered ; and, afraid
Of none but God, that persecuted band
Went forth and left no sign.　With God's right
　　hand
For shield and guide, their faith became sublime,
And persecution seemed earth's foulest crime.
The rain, and leaves strewn by the angry blast,
Washed out,. or hid all trace of where they
　　passed ;
And when the morning came, so fair and bright,
How such a day should follow such a night

Was theme of special wonder.   Earth and sky,
Bathed in the smile of Him who rules on high,
Seemed filled with peace and promise.   As a sign
It was accepted from the Power divine,
That the poor pilgrims should be onward led
As Israel's children, when with manna fed.
The autumn's frosts with curious chemic skill,
Had tinted every leaf on vale and hill,
Till all the forest seemed one fairy scene
Of gold and crimson, motley brown and green.
On ripened nuts the playful squir'l regaled ;
High in the air the lordly eagle sailed ;
And mocking birds, with sweet, melodious tongue,
Filled all the grove with their orchestral song.

    With grateful hearts the pilgrims onward sped;
A leafy carpet 'neath their feet was spread ;
And with one voice all nature seemed to bless
That lonely journey through the wilderness.
A common danger, which alike they shared ;
A common board, at which alike they fared ;
A common faith and trust, and that great love
Which binds on earth as in the realms above,
Filled them with perfect joy.   Each day they grew
Nearer and dearer.   Old, yet ever new,
The story of young hearts and young desires
Found fresh solution in those holy fires
Which stir the pulse to fond affection's glow,
And make man's world of happiness below.

    After three days of weary march thy came
Unto the lodge of Sacato, whose fame,

As a great Sachem, spread through all the land ;
His arm was strength : blood flowed at his com-
    mand.
Young Buffalo thus spoke :
                  " Great Chief, attend :—
We seek in thee protector, father, friend.
A brave am I.   This, my good sister, here,
And these fair strangers in thy realm appear
To claim thy kind and hospitable care :
Attend, great Chief, to our united prayer.
Brothers have proved unkind : We seek in you
A more than brother—friend and father too."
    Then the great Sachem thus :
                     " My heart is warm ;
My arms are open.   Fear no vengeful storm.
Thyself and friends are safe.   Sacato's word
Hath said it.   When was e'er Sacato heard
To say what was not so ?   Make this your home:
Be kindred with my people.   If you roam,
Come back again.   Who dares to do you harm
Shall feel the force and vengeance of my arm."
    A wigwam for the strangers was prepared,
And hospitality no token spared,
Of kind and princely welcome.   Ne'er had heav'n
Such cause of thankfulness to pilgrims given,
And ne'er did pilgrim band their souls pour out
In prayer more humble, grateful, and devout.
That "perfect love," which casteth out all fear,
Filled their true souls with its celestial cheer,
Till one in purpose, one in faith, they lent

Each to the other comfort and content.
  Two months passed fleetly by. 'Twas Christ-
    mas night.
The stars looked down with a fond, loving light,
And that same astral gem, whose guiding ray,
The wise men led to "where the young child lay,"
Held high his course in heaven.   The pilgrim
    priest
Had in his tent prepared a marriage feast.
A loving daughter and a loving son
Were, with his blessing, to be joined as one,
To those they dearly loved—those forest friends,
Whose faith had proved so true.   Two brides
    there were,
Each, in her way, superlatively fair ;
Like the wise virgins, each with oil supplied,
To greet the master's coming.   Side by side
They stood with those they loved, and with one
    breath
Vowed to be "faithful even unto death."
  Ah ! who can tell how soon o'er scenes most
    bright
Shadows may fall with gloom of darkest night—
How soon the purest, faithfulest, and best
May press the sod and with the weary rest !
God's ways, "past finding out," no man can
    know :
The foeman's wrath and the assassin's blow
May yield him praise, and kindest mercy prove :
Great are his judgments—greater still his love !

The Christmas watch was kept ; the midnight
    prayer
Went up to God, and his paternal care
Was asked for Christ's sake, on the joinéd lives
Of those fond husbands and those loving wives.
But hark—a rush—a yell—the knife—the brand—
Wielded by many a fierce and dusky hand,
Brought sudden death where, late, fond life and
    peace
Nursed brightest hopes, and looked for joy's in-
    crease.
That fearful scene of blood 'neath fury's sway,
Nor tongue, nor pen, nor pencil can portray.
Brief was the struggle. Wounded, scalped and
    bound ;
Their eyes plucked out and cast upon the ground ;
Their bodies mutilated ; burning darts
Fixed deep within their flesh. Still in their
    hearts
These Christians called on God, as did the
    Son !
" Forgive them, Father : Thy great will be
    done !"
    At length to spear and flame their bodies
    yield ;
The book of their sad martyrdom is sealed ;
And to eternal mansions in the skies,
From earthly hate, their pilgrim spirits rise.
    Swift as the eagle's flight the direful blow
Fell on the Christian hamlet, to o'erthrow

The fondest hopes e'er nursed.   But Vengeance
    stood—
The Nemesis of that wild, ancient wood—
With shafts already barb'd.   In God's fixed hour
E'en human wrath must vindicate His power.
Deep in the soil appeared a crimson stain,
And martyr-blood ne'er cried to heaven in vain !
The dusky triumph—the surprise by night—
May turn to mourning with the morrow's light,
When the red foeman the wild war-path seeks,
And a rude anger under honor speaks !
    Whose was the deed ?   The act itself pro-
      claimed
Its superstitious authors, and defamed
The very name of Brave.   Fanatic ire
Alone such deeds of darkness could inspire !
When first the pilgrims fled, pursuit had failed ;
Then the stern Seer against his warriors railed
Because with girdles scalpless they returned.
He mocked them ; called them women ; told how
    burned
The old Chief's ire, for children led astray
By pale-faced sorcery.   Then : " I'll lead the way,
And woe to all who fail !"   A trusty band
With that fierce Seer to counsel and command,
Again took up the trail.   A serpent's eyes,
When fixed in evil on some charmed prize,
Were, than the Seer's, less keen.   The serpent's
    guile
Could never equal his, and in his smile

There was a demon's power, a demon's pride,
That in self-confidence and hate relied.
With cunning and with patience he pursued
The cruel war-path through the peaceful wood,
Until, at length, his murderous success
Gave Christian martyrs to the wilderness.

    When to the ears of proud Sacato came
The tidings of the massacre, a flame
Of anger burned within him, and a vow
He registered to the Great Spirit : " Now,
Be this, my right arm, withered ; be my heart
Torn from my bosom; let my spirit start,
Dishonored to some hunting-ground of shame,
Where mocking fiends may scoff Sacato's name,
If swift extermination shall not fall
On the accursed tribe.   I sentence all
To die the death of dogs."
                Three thousand men
Sprang at Sacato's word from hill and glen,
And at the war-dance, by the bended bow,
And battle hatchet, swore that they would
    show
No mercy to those wild wolves of the wood,
Who roused their hate by such a deed of blood.
The war commenced ; fierce as Sacato's wrath,
Destruction followed the avenger's path,
Till the gorged raven and the vulture turned
With loathing from the bloody feast, and spurned
The proffered carnage.   Age nor sex was spared.
Infant and mother ; sire and maiden, shared,

With dusky braves, the death which bow and
    spear,
And fiery torture gave to war's career.
But Chief the Seer—Wild Serpent called—who
    planned
The murder of the pilgrims, and whose hand
Was reddest with their blood, felt the full flow
Of uncurbed vengeance.   Tortures sure but slow,
With every pang that savage nerves can feel,
Fed on his flesh and gnawed his heart of steel.
Bound to a tree ; a thousand spears of pine,
Ranged in fantastic figures, line o'er line,
Were thrust into his body.   Flame applied,
They blazed in pitchy fatness, till they fried
The living victim, so he writhed again
With all the stings of concentrated pain.
Thus lingeringly he lived for many an hour,
Until, at length, e'en torture lost its power,
And then he died—last of a fallen race—
With stern defiance branded on his face !

THE LAMENT.

[The following lines were suggested by the story of a somewhat aged wanderer whom the author met in a crowded city of the old world. Sorrow more than disease had left its traces on his cheek, and its palsy on his limbs, and it is presumed that long ere this he has passed to the object of his love in the spirit-land.]

My soul is lone,
As stepping o'er the stumbling blocks of Time,
And seeking happiness in many a clime,
I tread unknown,
'Mid granite solitudes and marble piles,
Where Poverty laments and Plenty smiles.

Oh ! there is pain
In that sad sense of loneliness, which steals
O'er the too conscious spirit, and reveals
The severed chain
Of Friendship, which in other days was bright
As Hope's young buds were bursting into light !

But distant far,
All sunny hours and early friends are now ;
For care has traced deep furrows on my brow ;
And many a scar,

The fadeless record of the foeman's strife,
Has made deformity my lot through life.

In early years,
When wealth embraced me, and when life's warm
    gush
Went bounding onward with a joyous rush,
    I nursed no fears
Foreshadowing a future, such as mine,
With care and grief recorded in each line.

I then did love,
And loving, was beloved ; but ah ! how soon
Death snatched my floweret in her spring's bright
    noon !
    Now, far above,
Her spirit blooms in ether realms again,
While mine droops here in penury and pain.

Oh ! how I wept
When she, the bright—the beautiful—the first,
For whom my soul's deep treasur'd love was nurst,
    Faded and slept !
And when the narrow house closed o'er her form,
I felt a calm more dreadful than the storm..

But soon I left
The dwelling of my fathers, and the home
Where, with my sweetest, I no more could roam :
    Of all bereft,

Save the sad recollections of a scene
Which could to me no more be clothed in green. .

  I sped away,—
And where the tocsin and the drum were heard ;
And where fame's clarion the spirit stirred,
  I sought to stay
The current of remembrance, and to blot
Her cherished image from my soul's sad thought.

  But ah ! no drop
From Lethean springs would check my wasting
  sigh,
Nor, till the fountains of my tears were dry
  Would they e'er stop
Their sad outpourings : and the midnight gale
Was oft wild witness of my mournful wail.

  I courted death—
Defied the fleshless monster—and would clasp
The pike and halbert with a phrensied grasp,
  But still my breath
Lingered within my nostrils :—none would try
The fatal steel on one who fought—*to die !*

  I left the field,
Sad, broken down in body as in mind,
Seeking relief ; but still, I failed to find
  Aught which could yield

The balm of quiet to my troubled soul,
Which, like the ocean, heaves with ceaseless roll.

I've sought for peace　　.
In distant lands and gay exotic climes ;
And revelry I've witnessed, sports, and crimes,—
　　But no release
Would my heart's jailor furnish.　All as yet
Have failed to teach my spirit to forget.

　　On life's dark verge
I stand in sadness, as in manhood's might,
When Hope's bright star first sank in sorrow's
　　night.
　　The ceaseless surge
Which speaks Eternity but whispers peace,
For in it all our earthly sorrows cease.

　　Welcome the day
When my o'erburdened spirit shall be free
From all the pains of earth-born misery !
　　When, far away,
I'll meet my life-lamented love on high,
To bid me welcome to Love's purer sky !

THE SONG OF COMMERCE.

I WAS born in the East, amid myrtle groves,
  Where flowerets forever bloom ;
I was fanned by the breeze which in fragrance
    roves
  O'er the gardens of Gul's perfume ;
And mine were the gold and the jewels, bright,
  Which were reared by a kingly hand,
As the joy and the pride of a people's might,
  In the Temple of Judah's land.

And mine were the cedars which waved on high,
  And mine were the ships of Tyre,
And mine were the breeze, which swept softly by,
  And the gale, which was loud in ire.
The costly ores from a thousand mines
  Were raised by my vassal train,
And the stately oaks and the mountain pines,
  For me, sought the distant main.

With the "staff of life" in my jewel'd hand,
  I have traced the majestic Nile—
I have stood where the Pyramid-mountains stand,
  And where Babel was wont to smile ;

I have passed o'er the lovely isles of Greece—
    I have dwelt in imperial Rome ;
And Carthage was mine, in her hours of peace,
    And in Venice I've sought a home.

I've lingered in Holland, and in my smile,
    Her fleets have sought every sea ;
I've circled around Albion's sea-girt isle,
    Then hied to " the land of the free ;"
And my standard now waves on Columbia's shore,
    Where the earth, from her teeming breast,
Hath gathered for me an unbounded store,
    On the plains of the "giant West."

Lakes, rivers, and " wooden walls " are mine,
    And those, who on Polar seas,
Seek treasures which I to the brave resign,
    Where the glittering icebergs freeze.
The world is mine, and my smile shall dwell
    With the peaceful of every land ;
The coffers I'll store, and the garners swell,
    Which the fearless and free have planned.

Then, hurra ! hurra ! for my fleets of pride—
    For my cities, a loud hurra !
I traverse the earth and the ocean wide,
    And naught shall impede my way.
The beautiful East and the boundless West,
    The chill and the burning clime,
Shall for aye rejoice in my high behest,
    Through the cycles of future time.

THE MOTHER'S LYRIC.

THREE there were, my boys, my trea-
    sures !
  Wallie first, my eldest born,
Like a dream of angel pleasures,
  Heralding eternal morn :
Gone to prove the soul's evangel,
Now a child, and now—an angel !
Change of being, gentle, blissful,
  'Twas when little Wallie died.

Georgie next, a laughing flower,
  Early blooming for the sky ;
Seeming, by some mystic power,
  Linked to fairer lands on high :
Proving still the soul's evangel,
Now a child, and now—an angel !
Change of being, gentle, blissful,
  'Twas when little Georgie died.

Then came Willie, latest, fleetest
  Faded he from earth away ;
Fading thus, he seemed the sweetest
  Flow'r that ever knew decay :

Still he proved the soul's evangel,
Now a child, and now—an angel!
Change of being, gentle, blissful,
'Twas when little Willie died.

NEW ORLEANS, 1856.

TO MOOSEHEAD LAKE.*

FAIR lake of the mountains, whose bright
    waters seem
To flow on in bliss like a beautiful dream ;
Now laving in gladness the hundreds of isles
Which gem thy broad surface and joy in thy
    smiles ;
To zephyr's soft music now dancing in pride,
As the hunter's light shallop the blue waves di-
    vide,
Or spreading in silver to mirror the skies,
And the forest-crowned mountains which round
    thee arise.

Fair lake of the mountains, proud Kineo's brow
For ages has frowned far above thee as now :
When the neighboring highlands, now sylvan and
    tame,
O'erflowed at their summits with lava and flame,

* Written during a visit to Maine in 1854.
    It is said that the Indians used in " the olden time " to
sacrifice their victims by throwing them over the perpen-
dicular cliffs of Mount Kineo.

And the Indian chieftains on Kineo met,
To pay to the war-god their terrible debt ;
Thy waters were witness ; and deep in thy caves
Are gathered the bones of the sacrificed " braves."

Fair lake of the mountains, romantic and wild
Are the scenes which in grandeur around thee
    have smiled,
Since poured forth in brightness from Deity's hand,
Thou hast looked on the charms of this mountain-
    ous land.
In sunshine, in shadow, in calm and in storm,
Thou hast varying beauties no change can deform;
And thy sons and thy daughters, may they ever be
As fair as thy waters, as pure and as free !

INNOCENCE.

TO ——.

THOUGH fair were the earliest bowers of
    love,
  With their beautiful blossoms of every hue,
Though pure was the incense of Eden's grove,
    Which on zephyr-pinions in fragrance flew,—
Yet fairer and purer, and sweeter still,
    Than Eden's flow'rs or fragrant air,
Was the guileless charm-and the vestal will,
    Which Innocence gave unto all things there.

But the serpent came, and the charm was lost,
    And briars and thorns in the garden grew,
And Innocence, frighted and tempest-tost,
    For a place of rest o'er the waters flew.
Like an angel-spirit too pure for earth,
    It sometimes wandered from star to star,
But it still would sigh for its place of birth—
    For its native Eden, afar, afar !

And then it would seek in some spicy grove,
    A spot where the daisies had blushed unseen,
Where it could, mid the flowers in freedom rove,
    And the children of Flora could hail it queen.

Still, still for a temple more purely bright,
   As a wandering Peri again 'twould roam,
And it ne'er found that temple of love and light,
   'Till it found in thy breast an abiding home.

THE LEGEND OF RELLE ISLE.

AMONG the many places in Newfoundland remarkable for their romantic sublimity, Belle Isle, in Conception Bay, is especially interesting. The rocks on the eastern end of the island are most beautifully fluted out by the hammerless masonry of the ever-working waves, and towering up some hundreds of feet into the air, they present no imperfect imitation of the sublimest specimens of architectural grandeur. Standing on two promontory projections of the overhanging cliff, may be seen a male and a female figure, perfect in shape, as if cut out of the solid rock by the delicate hand of the sculptor. But there the artist never stood—the shelving rock would mock at his attempt to scale it, and the sublime proportions of the statues could never be copied by his hand. Thus it is that the freaks of Nature are more wonderful at times than the proudest triumphs of Art.

A traditionary legend speaks of these figures as being the tutelar angels of the Isle, and once its sole inhabitants. The place was then a very paradise of delight, and so enraptured were they

with its beauties that they fixed a bell on the end
of it which fronts the setting sun, which would
ring a peal, melodiously enchanting at morn, at
mid-day, and at the approach of night; but
whenever wandering spirits agitated the air or the
surrounding waters by their motions, it gave a
tone so wild, discordant, and frightful as to urge
the intruders hastily from the loved domain. This
bell, with its clapper, may still be seen near the
site it originally occupied ; but an invisible guardian protects them from the polluted tread and
scrutinizing examination of man.

In course of time, tradition proceeds to say,
its inhabitants made wings to take their loved
island to the land of the gods. The gods, infuriate at their presumption, about the midnight
that ushered in May-morning of the year, sent a
sword of fiery flame which clipped the monster
wings just trembling on the eve of motion, and
drove the aspiring angels over the island's eastern
brow. The rocks on that portion of the island
being enchanted, were no sooner touched by the
falling victims of ambition than the once happy
pair were converted into marble, as solid as the
rock against which they clung. And there they
have ever since been ; and on every annual return
of the hour that they fell, the echoes of the Isle
are awakened by a strain of music from each,—
the only vestiges they retain of their once heavenly powers.

The male sings thus :

I HAVE roamed, I have roamed, as the lord of the
 Isle,
And alone I have lived in my loved one's smile ;
I have braved, I have braved the celestial ire,
And the sword that was edged with electric fire ;
And my yearly song, from the marble steep
I sing, when the ocean is lulled to sleep.
Still, still its burden my loved one's smile,
And the verdant plains of my beautiful Isle.

On my wave-washed cliff I have stood, I have
 stood,
Since the deluge rolled its resistless flood :—
A thousand nations have passed away
Since the echoes awoke to my yearly lay :—
The gods of the ocean in worship meet
In the billowy waters beneath my feet,
But they're naught when compared with my lov'd
 one's smile
And the Eden plains of my beautiful Isle.

The female sings thus :

Awake, O awake ! to my midnight song :
The maiden who lists will live happy and long.
And the youth who attends to my yearly lay,
With the roses of pleasure I'll scatter his way.

I have lived in my Isle when unending spring
Would its scented flow'rets around me fling ;
And I've revelled in bliss, while my loved one's
    smile
Still hailed me queen of my beautiful Isle.

The sportive mermaids around me play !
And the ocean-nymphs with enchanting lay
Stil cheer me onward from year to year,
With the echoing song which to me is dear ;
And dear are the strains of celestial bands,
And the myriad songs of Elysian lands,
But dearer by far is my loved one's smile,
And the Eden plains of my beautiful Isle.

THE WIND-GOD'S SONG.

IN my car of clouds, through the " upper deep,"
    I sweep o'er the trembling sea ;
And the billowy surges, aroused from sleep,
    Keep time to my minstrelsy.

A thousand ships from a thousand climes
    Await my uncertain breath,
Where, freighted with treasures, and hopes, and
      crimes,
    They would steer by the shoals of death :

But my ire, aroused by the vassal train,
    I give, to the tempest, birth,
And I laugh, in my might, at the sons of pain
    As they sigh for the solid earth.

The cry of sorrow aloud is heard !
    The shriek, and the dying wail—
The ships have sunk !—the waves are stirr'd
    In the dance, to the midnight gale.

Now I breathe a calm o'er the " yeast of waves,"
　　And the watery warrings cease ;
And deep, in the mermaid's ocean caves,
　　The mariner sleeps in peace.

And afar, afar, o'er the desert land
　　I pass in my fleecy car ;
And the pestilence bows to my high command,
　　And the Siroc is sent afar.

And now I come with the sweets of spring,
　　And the leaf and the flow'ret's bloom
Break forth, in the warmth of my zephyr-wing
　　From the chill of their wintry tomb.

And now, again, through the summer air,
　　I breathe on the fevered brow ;
And a joyous welcome awaits me where
　　The faint and the feeble bow.

And now, to the bowers of love I hie,
　　And I bend unto lips of bliss,
(From my viewless home in the changeful sky),
　　Which an angel might stoop to kiss.

And I pass o'er the fields of ripening corn,
　　The children of toil to cheer ;
And in joy, at the fullness of Plenty's horn,
　　I speed in my wild career.

A MOTHER'S QUESTIONINGS.

WHERE art thou gone, my Henry ?
    O, I could not think that thou
Wouldst leave us, as the sunlight leaves,
    At eve, the mountain's brow.
Thy presence was a constant joy—
    A ray of life and light—
And now thou'rt gone, the world seems filled
    With Absence and with Night !

    Go ask the wailing waters,
      Gentle mother, they can tell ;
    There's speech within their darkened flow,
      To thee, perchance a knell !
    Amid their coral colonnades
      His form was gently laid,
    And well he sleeps, as if his couch
      By loving hands were made.

I've spoken to the waters,
    But they rolled along in pride,
All heedless of my questionings,
    And not a wave replied—

Save in sad, hollow murmur-tones
  Which seemed like echoes dread,
Of lov'd ones lost, forever lost,
  Till seas gave up their dead.

    Then question thou the heavens,
      And the radiant orbs, which sweep
    In music and in brilliancy
      Through the celestial deep.
    The sea but holds the casket, frail—
      The sky has claimed the gem,
    And now it sparkles in the light
      Of God's own diadem.

O come to me, my Henry,
  Come in thy angelic guise,
And to my earthly questionings
  Give heavenly replies.
It is his voice—I know it well—
  It comes to bless and cheer—
My Henry lives the better life :
  Farewell to grief and fear !

NEW ORLEANS, *October*, 1856.

The above lines were written by request, on the death of
a pupil in the New Orleans Public Schools, who was acci-
dentally knocked overboard from a vessel, and drowned in
the Gulf of Mexico.

TO THE MAGNOLIA.

GEM of the forest, delicately bright,
    Spotless and pure as Eden's fairest flower ;
That comest with thy treasures to delight
    The fairy halls of Love's encircling bower.

In the gay world, methinks, I've heard it said,
    That there were mysteries of Floral lore,
Recorded on fair flow'ret-leaves which, read,
    By ardent lovers, caused them to adore.

And oft have I, with wrapt attention, sought
    For the full knowledge of each gentle page
Which warms the soul with joyousness when
        taught,
    And gives a higher wisdom to the sage.

And thou, sweet forest flow'r, hast always seemed
    The best translatress of Affection's sigh ;
For warmth, and truth, and purity have beamed
    From the warm sun which lights thy native sky.

Canst thou " translate the poetry of hearts ?"
　O ! whisper, then, the story of my flame—
The dream of bliss its silent thought imparts
　Its soft devotion to one cherished name.

And I will bless thee for the kindly deed,
　And own thy balmy breath and gentle swell
All musical and eloquent, to plead
　The deep emotions words can never tell.

HOPE—A Fragment.

'MID the glittering gems, so profusely strewed,
    O'er the boundless wilds of Infinitude,
One star, of a lovelier, purer sheen
Than its sister lights could boast, was seen :
But a cloud appeared ; and I looked with pain
On the shrouding gloom of its sable train,
As that chosen star with the silv'ry ray
In its deep embrace seemed to fade away.
All sadly I looked ; and a darkening shade
O'er my world of thought like a demon strayed,
For the choir which shouted Creation's hymn
In that partial blackness had all grown dim.
But now, through the silence of gloom was heard
The reviving tone of a whispered word—
'Twas *Hope*—and then, dropping a grateful tear,
I knew that my star would again appear.

  * * * * * *

'Mid the flowers that smiled in a garden dell,
And honeyed the dews as they softly fell,
And anointed the breeze, ever wont to stray
With its cooling charm at the close of day,
I sat ;—and a rapture, unknown before,
Seemed roused in the midst of that Floral store,

As a flower, of flowers the fairest queen,
In that beautiful sisterhood first was seen.
With its fragrance so sweet, and its tints so rare,
No rival blossom could e'er compare ;
And I gazed with a new and strange delight,
As the sun swept on to his couch of night.
Long ere I had ended my fond survey,
"The glorious king" of declining day
Had 'missioned his heralds to softly close
The blossoms which joyed in a fond repose ;
And I sighed, as lovers alone can do,
When my beautiful flower was lost to view.

But Hope, forever a constant friend,
With words of promise drew near to lend
That soothing light which can bless and cheer—
That guide to thought in its dark career ;
And then, I knew that my longing sight
Should again be blessed with a morrow's light—
That my flower again, as a queenly bride,
Should appear in the blush of its maiden pride.
Then bright, through the shadows which would
　　　destroy,
Beamed the sunlight promise of future joy.

LAST ISLAND.

[On the 10th of August, 1856, a hurricane swept over a
portion of the Gulf of Mexico, and entirely submerged Last
Island, one of the group of sand islands stretching along the
southern coast of Louisiana.   The island was a favorite
summer resort for planters and their families, and, when
visited by the storm, had a temporary population of about
four hundred souls, chiefly from adjacent parishes.   Of this
number more than half were drowned, and every building
on the island was swept away by the fury of the storm.]

A STRANGE wild spot
Was that "Last Island" in the Mexic sea,
Where winds and waves and wild birds wandered
    free ;
        And there was naught
But promised joy for those who gathered there
To seek in summer ease divorce from care.

        The fair and young,
The wise, the eloquent, the true, the brave,
Found health and music in each rolling wave ;
        And wild harps, strung
To softer minstrelsy, essayed to please
By peans gentle as the gentlest breeze.

Oh, what delight
It was, at eve, to wander round the isle
When all was golden with Sol's parting smile !
And when young Night—
Her zone enriched with Venus and with Mars—
Arrayed her bosom with her wealth of stars !

Lovers there were
Who thus would wander, and who thus were
    blest ;
While e'en the foam-bells on each wavelet's crest,
As if to share
In love's Elysium, kissed the sounding shore,
And with prismatic glories strewed it o'er.

Morn to the isle
Came with a rosy flush. The balmy air
Breathed of delights which it were bliss to share,
And Nature's smile
Never more true, and ne'er more kindly seemed
Since first in light it on creation beamed.

But soon a change
Spread darkling o'er the heav'ns. The sea-gulls'
    cry
Gave note, prophetic, of some danger nigh,
As with wild rage
They swept the air, and sought, perchance, to flee
The coming fury of the wind and sea.

A heaving surge,
With all a storm's deep prelude in its roar,
Began to beat along the island's shore ;
  And still did urge
Each wave its fellow with resistless force,
And hurried onward in its headlong course.

  And now the gale
Burst in its might that lonely isle upon.
The hurricane, the hurricane swept on,
  And a wild wail,
That seemed the knell of hope, and shriek and
  sigh
And wilder prayers assailed the stormy sky.

  Gods ! what a sight !
When the mad waves o'erwhelmed the troubled
  Strand,
And mingled in their yeast that isle of sand ;
  And in their might
Bore piecemeal off, as trophies of their foam,
The strong-bound mansion and the humbler home.

  Amid the strife
Of raging waters and of raging wind
What sure protector shall weak woman find ?
  And childhood's life,
'Tis as a bubble, where ascends " the cry
Of the strong swimmer in his agony !"

O, cruel wave !
Why didst thou bear from a fond lover's arms
His fair affianced one, and of her charms
    So fiercely rave ?
And when thou hadst her living form caressed,
Why didst thou hide her corse within thy breast ?

    But on, O Death !
Thou hast thy harvest now ; bestrew thy path
With the dark records of thy wasting wrath,
    For fleeting breath,
Though linked to immortality, must yield
To such an enemy on such a field !

    Yet triumph not,
For when what seemeth human life is gone,
The mortal immortality puts on—
    A blissful lot !
And meets a welcome from an angel band,
In songs that breathe of the celestial land.

    No storms are there,
In that far country of supreme delight,
To which the soaring spirit takes its flight,
    But all is fair
As seraph dreams of some supernal isle,
Bathed in the light of God's eternal smile.

    A steamer's wreck,
Imbedded in the island's shifting sand,
Forms a last refuge for a broken band ;

And on her deck
Together cling, washed by the 'whelming spray,
The few who mourn the many swept away.

What tears were shed—
What perilous attempts were made to save
The fair and helpless from the hostile wave—
What lovers, wed
By the stern storm's espousal, heard their knell
In the loud thunder's crash 'twere vain to tell !

Night came anon ;
O, clingers to the wreck, a fearful night !
The lightning's fitful flash your only light !
Wives, children gone !
Your hearts and hearths left desolate ! yet o'er
The hurricane still sweeps and asks for more !

So passed away
A night of anguish on the stranded wreck.
Morn came, the fury of the storm to check ;
And as the day
Advanced, the waters fell, and the lone isle,
E'en in its ruin, seemed to wear a smile !

Along the strand,
Care-worn and sad, with slow and mournful tread,
The living wander, searching for the dead !
For those who planned
With them, but yestermorn, fair-fashioned schemes
Of life and bliss, now fled, like morning dreams !

And here and there,
Stretched on the sand or rolling with the wave,
Some dear, familiar form demands a grave :
The young, the fair,
The servant and his master, side by side—
For death, the robber, robbed them e'en of pride !

Sad was the task
To give them fitting sepulture—to hide
Its fairest trophies from the moaning tide,
Which seemed to ask,
With hollow, dirge-like cadence, what had led
These tearful mourners thus to claim its dead !

But far away,
Down in the depths, or to some distant shore,
Or on some life-supporting fragment, o'er
The water's play,
The lost were chiefly borne.   How few again
Shall ever mingle in the walks of men !

Another night—
A night of storm, and still another day,
A day of anxious longing wore away,
Before the sight
Of a strong steam-urged bark announced relief,
And joy again gleamed o'er the brow of grief.

Hail to the saved !
What welcome now awaits them ! rapture wild
Is that fond mother's, when she clasps her child

Who fearless braved
The war of waters—form enclasped to form—
And hurried questionings—the storm? the storm?

Strange answer came :
Absence and Silence told a tale of dread—
Spoke of the loved—the lost—the early dead,
For words were tame
To tell how desolation breathed upon
The isle, and its inhabitants were gone !

NEW ORLEANS, *August*, 1856.

THE SHADOW ON THE PILLOW.

[A highland soldier, who had been severely wounded in battle, and whose life was saved by the careful nursing and gentle ministrations of Florence Nightingale—the heroine of the Crimea—said, on being asked how he felt towards his preserver, that his gratitude was too great for words, and the only mode he had of giving vent to his feelings, was by kissing her shadow when it fell on his pillow as she passed through the ward on her nightly visit.—*Foreign Paper.*]

AMONG the wounded, on his couch,
 The Highland soldier lay,
And from his wounds the tide of life
 Was ebbing fast away,
When o'er him bent a gentle form,
 To hear his dying tale—
'Twas that angel of the Hospital,
 Fair Florence Nightingale.

" Ah, me !" he cried—that soldier stern—
 " My wife and children dear,
So far, so very far away,
 While I am dying here.
Great God ! and must I perish thus ;
 And shelterless and lone,
Leave those whose love is more than life—
 My beautiful—my own ?"

" Cease, soldier !" said a gentle voice,
  " For He, who rules on high,
Can hear as well the widow's wail
  As the young raven's cry.
Trust in His strength, as thou art weak,
  And let thy prayers ascend
To Him, the widow's surest stay—
  The orphan's kindest friend.

" And haply, soldier, we may yet,
  With God's good aid, restore
Thee to thy wife and little ones
  As hale as heretofore ;
And O, what swelling, thankful hearts—
  What joy there will be then,
To brighten up the soldier's home
  Within his Highland glen !"

Like dew upon the bruised reed—
  Like light to dungeons dark—
Or like the dove, with olive boughs,
  Returning to the ark,
Came those kind, gentle, hopeful words
  Unto the soldier's ear,
With prophet-dreams of health restored,
  And home's reviving cheer.

With skillful hands the angel nurse
  Poured oil and wine upon
The soldier's agonizing wounds,
  Until their pang was gone ;

And still she nursed him tenderly
 Through months, which glided by,
Before health bloomed upon his cheek
 Or brightened in his eye.

Ah, gentle one, 'tis thine to bless !
 Thy mission is divine ;
And rays from Heaven's mercy seat
 Upon thy pathway shine.
There's healing in thy woman's hand,
 And, in thy woman's heart,
A fount of gentleness, whose flow
 No impulse gains from art.

And, soldier, say—what thoughts arise
 When she, thy nurse, appears ?
The soldier turned upon his couch,
 And, checked by manly tears,
He answered, " words are weak to tell ;
 Her shadow seems like light,
And I kiss it as she walks the ward
 To cheer the sick by night !"

New Orleans, *November*, 1856.

THE EAGLE AND THE DOVE.

[The following legend was related to the author at one of the "Posts" of the Hudson Bay Company. The "Eagle" and the "Dove" belonged to a tribe of mountain Indians, in Lower Canada, among whom a superstition, relative to the deification of celebrated warriors, was prevalent. The religious opinions of the mountain Indians differ in many respects, as well as in this particular, from those commonly received by the American tribes.]

BENEATH, swept on the mighty stream,
    Above, the maiden stood,
And calmly fell the moon's pale beam
    Upon that ancient wood.
And graceful seemed that forest maid,
    As in the checkered light,
To the stern battle-god she prayed
    For succor in the fight.

Her lover was an Eagle Brave,
    By danger compassed round,
Though for each wound his arrows gave,
    A foe would bite the ground ;
But she, with woman's sympathy,
    And woman's fearless love,
Would read the words of mystery
    The stars had traced above.

An earthen mound was by her side,
  Within, the dust was laid
Of him—the dead—the deified,
  To whom that maiden prayed ;
And long she prayed before the god
  In giant-guise appeared,
And noiseless o'er the velvet sod,
  With his high hand upreared.

He moved,—and pointing to the sky,
  With accents cold and stern,
He said, "your chief in victory
  To you can ne'er return.
The star which gleamed along his path,
  With its protecting light,
Is darkened by a cloud of wrath
  Which shadows o'er the fight :

" Your loosened spirit can alone
  Ascend, and roll away
The cloud which o'er that star is thrown,
  To intercept its ray.
But if the shadow still remains
  Around your Eagle-Brave,
His arm no more its strength retains—
  His bow no more can save."

" Then his shall be the victory,
  As his has been the right,
If death and darkness shrouding me
  Can send him life and light "—

She said—and with a fawn-like bound,
    She plunged beneath the stream ;
And coldly where the maid was drowned
    Still slept the moon-lit beam.

But soon a cloud was rolled away
    From the o'erarching sky,
And glittering with peerless ray,
    A star appeared on high :
Again an arm, as erst, was strong—
    Again a bow was bent—
But little knew the victor-throng
    By whom success was lent.

And now the storm of war is stilled,
    And as its thunders cease,
For victor warriors are filled
    The cups of love and peace :
And many a maiden's song of praise
    'Mid forest-vines, is heard,
As joyous as when upward strays
    The music of a bird.

But she, the bird of sweetest tone—
    The Eagle-lover's pride—
Is silent, and the Dove alone
    Is distant from his side.
And long the victor-chieftain mourned
    The silence of that voice
Which never to his ear returned,
    To gladden and rejoice.

And ne'er again his battle-spear,
  Or shaft-impelling bow,
Did onward urge a stern career,
  To triumph o'er a foe.
And when, at length, the chieftain died,
  Full oft, at close of day,
Two spirit-shadows, side by side,
  Were seen in love to stray.

LINES TO ———.

A S when the softly wooing breeze,
 In fondness, sweeps the sylvan lyre,
And, mid the fragrant orange trees,
 A sound as from an angel choir,
In music, tells its lov'd career,
 While all the odor-sweets of spring,
A sisterhood, forever dear,
 Attend, on zephyr's viewless wing :

So, to my ear thy harp's rich sound
 Comes, breathing melody's perfume ;
For ne'er was sweeter music found
 To stray o'er Eden's virgin bloom :
And my poor harp, all lone, and sad,
 Would fondly echo back the strain,
If it thy purer ear could glad,
 And bid thee wake those tones again.

But fate forbids.—The blissful dream
 Inspired by thy minstrelsy
Must pass—for never, never deem
 That I could bring down cares on thee !

O ! would'st thou "cling ?"—fond creature !—
    thou
Art far too innocent and fair,
Before the storms of life to bow,
    And with me all their perils dare.

Would I could wed thee !—but the thought
    Is madness !—I will not repine—
Though all the treasures of my lot—
    My heart and harp shall aye be thine :
To see thee fade, I could not bear,
    So thou shalt be my "spirit-bride !"
Nor time, nor misery, nor care
    Shall ever force thee from my side.

LINES ON GEORGE COOKE, ESQ.

[The following lines, humbly inscribed to the nearest and dearest friend of the deceased, were written in memory of George Cooke, Esq., distinguished alike for his talents as an artist, and his virtues as a man. Mr. Cooke departed this life on 26th March, 1849, at his residence in the city of New Orleans.]

THE sun of genius smiled upon his way,
  And warmed his soul with its creative beams,
While painted fancies round him seemed to play,
  To bless and beautify his waking dreams.

Then glowed the canvas with the warmth of life,
  Then Beauty owned the magic of his will,
As the fond mother and the loving wife
  Immortal seemed—the triumph of his skill.

The wasting ruin and the floating wreck—
  The suff'ring form—the madness of despair—
The bower which Floral offerings bedeck—
  The lover-hero, doomed to "do and dare"—

·All these have, 'neath his pencil's magic touch,
  Through the dim vista of far-distant years,
Cast a reflected light, which, Fame shall much
  Delight to cherish, as the future nears.

And while Fame waits on Genius; Friendship,
    Love,
  Awake in Memory the tear of joy,
As soaring Faith attends his course above,
  To where his higher "talents" claim employ.

RELIGION, POETRY AND MUSIC.

[Written for a Lady's Album, in which Religion, Poetry
and Music were beautifully represented by an appropriate
trio of figures.]

RELIGION.

WHEN sorrow's mantle shadows o'er the
    soul,
Religion spreads around her holy calm
Which dissipates the tempest clouds, that roll
    O'er troubled waters as the spirit's balm :—
And when the vanities of life shall end,
    And earth's endearments have forever fled,
Religion then, Hope's Heaven arch'd bow shall
    bend
    Above the silent " Cities of the Dead."

POETRY.

The poet's fancy is a breathing stream
    Which gathers incense from each flow'ry way—
As full of freshness as love's virgin dream,
    And wild and sportive as an untamed fay;

It binds in flowing wreaths the burning thought—
  It plays with the wing'd lightning thro' the sky—
It laughs at Desolation's tramp ;—and naught
  Can tame its wildness, or its sources dry.

MUSIC.

The voice of music, like an angel's breath,
  Now, full of gentle sweetness, soars above
The fields of Fancy, from which bards enwreathe
  The kindred flowers of Purity and Love !
And *now*, it takes a spirit-stirring tone
    Which nerves the senses fraught with martial
      strife,
And rolls wild ardor through the " living zone "
  Which circles round the sterner paths of life.

ADDRESS.*

[Written for the occasion of the Firemen's Annual Benefit in the Variétés Theatre, and respectfully dedicated to the Firemen of the Consolidated City of New Orleans.]

GOD bless the Firemen !—You my constant
    friends,
From whose warm hearts the generous prayer as-
    cends,
Can give the orison an incense wing ⸮
As soft and fragrant as the breeze of spring.
God bless the Firemen !—let the echoes rise,
In truthful breathings through the ambient skies.

When in the " noon of night " the loud alarm
Startles the sleeper, and the voice of harm,
Spoken by iron tongues, gives note that, led
By fiends of flame, empanoplied with dread,
The spirit of destruction is abroad,
Fierce with the fury of a demon-god !

* This Address was recited by that gifted actress, Mrs.
C. Howard, so long a favorite at the Variétés, in 185–.

Whose then the task to meet the raging foe ?
And whose, to lay the fell destroyer low ?
Needless it were to answer.   All can tell,
For all the Fireman's daring know full well.

  Still, onward still, Destruction's lurid tide
Rolls with the gale, its vassel and its guide.
Raging and surging on, from roof to roof,
As if it claimed for its own mad behoof,
Art's choicest triumphs ; while the builder's skill
Is naught compared with its wild, wayward will.

  Now the proud column and the strong bound
      arch
Crumble and fall beneath the onward march
Of the fierce waves of flame, which, rising, seem
To realize some hell-engendered dream.

  But tired, at length, of inorganic prize,
For nobler sacrifice the fire-fiend cries—
'Tis life he asks—nor longer will he tread
On things alone, inanimate and dead.
Ho ! let the triumphs of the loom be brought,
And golden gifts, and treasure tomes of thought !
He mocks them all, and marks them with his hate,
And still he asks for Life ! for Life !—too late,
Perchance, will be the Fireman's saving arm
To free from danger and to shield from harm.

Here in an attic's flame-encircled height,
A little child, a thing of life and light,
Slumbers, unconscious of the danger near—
Its angel mother never taught it fear.
'Twine as ye list, wild wreathes of glaring flame,
Ye cannot check the Fireman's noble aim—
He rears the ladder—scales the tottering wall—
To save that infant's life, he perils all !
And oh ! success his saving arm attends—
Heaven will befriend him, who that child be-
    friends !

Then is it strange that beauty's gentle breast
Swells with wild heavings, as, when dream-
    caressed,
Whene'er the Fireman's noble deeds are told—
And love is his reward—more prized than gold ?
In Beauty's breast 'tis e'er the Fireman's aim
To kindle, not annihilate a flame ;
For in that breast, and in that Beauty's worth,
Are meet rewards for more than deeds of earth.
So may it ever be—let woman's eye
Light on the brave to nobly do, or die !

LINES.

[Written on the bursting of the boilers of a large steam
mill in Nova Scotia.]

THE sun beamed high in Heaven. With
    tireless arm
  The steam-urged engine played its constant
    round,
And moved with iron-life, as if a charm
  Of wizard spell was in its motion bound,
And lava-like its lymph-blood boiled, and found
  Its madd'ning way through each conflicting vein;
And foaming, murmured with unearthly sound
  Against all those who would attempt to rein
Its madden'd pulse, or giant force, for fame or gain.

But soon, determined not to brook control
  Nor be the slave of man's ambitious might,
It burst its iron vestment, as a soul
  Bursts its dark prison for the realms of light.
A thousand scattered fragments in their flight,

And the loud thunder of the startled air,
Aroused the fears of each attendant wight,
And many sought their fellows in despair,
And feared for each that death which all might
    dread to share.

For mountain heaps of masonry and brick
    Were strewn around them as a vengeful rain
Of heav'n directed fury : fast and thick
    Fell the huge fragments ; and the shriek of
      pain
Was heard ; and wond'ring that they were not
      slain,
    The living found the wounded and the dead ;
The mangled body and the scattered brain
    Arrest their steps ; and if they further tread,
The scalded man appears mid devastation's spread.

THE MAY FLOWER OF THE NORTH.*

[In imitation of the Persian.]

I.

BEAUTIFUL flower, why dost thou nestle lowly amid the snows ? The chill breeze of the North is upon thee, and though the green leaves of thy native vine gather protectingly round, they cannot gladden and warm thee as could the softer smiles of a sunny clime. Beautiful flower, all lonely and hidden thou lyest now; but if thy petals were expanded where a kinder sun warms a land' of unfading spring, then mightest thou stand erect among the beautiful children of Flora, and claim, thy worship of the fragrant sisterhood.

II.

Close and more closely nestled the beautiful flower beneath the emerald leaves which preserved their freshness through all the storms of winter, and grateful for the shelter they afforded, it gave

* The May flower is the political emblem of the Author's native land, Nova Scotia.

its incense to the tiny bowers which decorated
the hillock upon which it grew. A faint voice
from the snow-margined hillock was heard, and it
seemed to say : " I sigh not for the land of unfading spring, nor the worship of a gaudy and
haughty sisterhood. In a warmer clime the hot
sun would scorch me with its withering beams,
and more proud and queenly flow'rets would look
on me with contempt. Here I am first, and
fondest, and dearest, being first—there, amid
continuous bloom I could not be first, and lowly
and unknown, I would be trampled on and despised." Then fainter and fainter became the voice
till its sounds were no longer heard.

III.

Beautiful flower, there is wisdom in thy voice
and instruction in thy leaves, and the child of
man who listens to thy teachings will learn to be
humble and content. Though the perfume and
the beauty of the orange blossom are thine, yet
where the bloom of the orange sheds its fragrance
on the air, thou mightest indeed be overlooked in
thy lowliness and trampled on in neglect ; and all
unknown in thy modest beauty and humble worth,
thy sweetness would be wasted and thy blushes
be unseen. Beautiful flower, I thank thee for the
lesson thou hast given, and O, that I may profit
by thy teachings !

FRAGMENT OF A POEM.

[Written on visiting "Signal Hill," at the entrance of the
harbor of St. John's, Newfoundland.]

BENEATH, upon the harbor's silv'ry tide,
   The white-winged messengers of Commerce
glide,
Whose banners, trembling in the unseen breeze,
Mark whence they hail—these wonders of the
   seas.
   We turn—unnumbered beauties gild the scene;
In the rich rays of evening's rosy sheen,
The distant hills with burnished splendor rise
To kiss the cloud-robed spirit of the skies.
Nearer, the fields, whose cultivated soil
Shows the reward of industry and toil,
Bare their broad bosoms to the king of light,
Who, smiling, lingers as he bids—*good night!*
While nearer still, the limpid lake is spread,
O'er which the dancing zephyrs lightly tread ;
And into which the purling streamlets flow,
In their bright journey to the seas below.
And here is reared the adamantine rock,
Whose rugged crest ascends aloft to mock

Th' electric blaze—the thunder's dreadful roar,
And ocean's surge, which sounds along the shore.
    Seaward we turn our gaze—and from the steep,
The brown-sail'd " Jack,"* is seen to skim the
        deep ;
She bears the fisher, hardy, strong and brave,
And ocean-treasures, drawn from 'neath the wave;
By day, she breasts the billowy foam ;—at night,
She marks her course with phosphorescent light.
    Aloft, on buoyant wing, the sea-birds rise,
In trackless circles through the ambient skies,
And round the proud ship course the watery
        plain,
And mock her tardy movements in disdain.
    Here too, the soldier, with his measured pace,
With form erect, and with becoming grace,
Strides to and fro, and glancing o'er the foam,
Thinks of his early love !—his early home !
    And here we stand ; and ne'er shall be erased
These pictur'd scenes on mem'ry's pages traced,
Varied in beauty—wildly, boldly grand—
By Nature's pencil drawn, by Nature planned.
Amid these scenes may knowledge rear her head,
Her brightest lustre here may virtue shed,
And here may bards of brighter genius rise,
" For souls may ripen in these Northern skies."

        * A fishing-boat, so called in Newfoundland.

WRECK OF THE NAUTILUS.*

WAR on the waters! now the Cyclone's breath
Rouses the waves in the wild dance of death,
Tears off their crests, as revolutions tear
The crowns from Kings.   There's fury in the air,
Assuming horrent shapes, which madly sweep,
With demon cries, across the tortured deep.

Woe to the mariner! his oak-ribbed bark
No more can serve as a protecting ark!
Mastless and rudderless she drifts, a wreck,
While the fierce billows thunder on her deck,
Still clamorous for victims!   Woe to thee,
Thou peopled plaything of the raging sea!

Here cling the brave, whom storms cannot appal,
And there, the timid, who all vainly call,
In prayers, fear-prompted, for some swift relief,
Still mingling with the waves their tears of grief.

O, soaring Hope, thy gentle wings must fail
When scathful ruin rides upon the gale !
Man's puny might is powerless to save ;
For regal Neptune has prepared a grave,
All coral gemm'd, down in his purple deep,
And summoned all his Nereids to weep !

High and still higher rolls the mountain surge ;
Fierce and still fiercer angry tempests urge
Its onward sweep : it comes !—it comes !—be-
    ware !—
Whom, in its 'whelming fury, will it spare ? .
O'erturned and torn, a thing of broken pride,
The wreck is swallowed by the hungry tide,
And, as it disappears, wild prayers and cries
Of concentrated agony arise.
O man, still clinging to that bubble, life,
Why art thou still with destiny at strife ?
What boots thy frantic struggles ?   Death is
    nigh—
Yield, yield and learn : *it is not hard to die !*

Some sink at once within the roaring sea,
To rise, the heirs of immortality ;
While others, battling with the billows, gain
A few sad moments more of life and pain.
Thus, one by one, the victims disappear,
Till all save two are gone, two strugglers, near
Each other clinging to a floating tree,
Thrown in their way by chance or destiny.

The storm has spent its fury : now again
Bright skies are mirrored in the glassy main,
And the two seamen, on their friendly pine,
Voyage along in safety o'er the brine.
Their bark, of roots fantastic is possessed,
Wreathed in the form of a gigantic nest,
Where, in the wilds of ocean solitude,
Some monster bird has nursed her callow brood.

Here nestling, hopeful seemed the twain at first,
But soon came hunger and unceasing thirst
To rack them into torture. Oh ! what pain
To be thus starving on the wat'ry plain !
To hope till hope assumes the guise of death,
And torture is increased with every breath !
Thus days and days were spent, till phantoms
     rose
With ghastly horrors to augment their woes;
Strange shapes flit past that mocked them as
     they flew ;
Strange sounds seemed uttered by some demon
     crew,
And all seemed strange, and terrible, and dread
As fiendish revels round the unshrived dead !
E'en the wing'd fish, in fond and sportive flight,
Were birds of evil omen to their sight ;
And the fair nautilus, with silken sail,
Was but the prophet of some rising gale.
Down in the deep what monster forms drew nigh,
With eyes of fire ; and skeletons swam by,

Like mocking deaths, which seemed, with bony
    hand,
To point new terrors in some viewless land.
Surrounded thus with every form of woe
That shipwrecked man was ever doomed to know,
One of the two leaped madly in the tide
To cool his burning brow ; he sank, and died !

The other still lived on, if it be life,
When every breath with agony is rife,
And when, with waning strength, to know and feel
Has more of pang than torture's racking wheel.
He was of Ethiop blood and stalwart frame,
And lived, he knew not why.   No honor'd name
And wealth of hopes were his; still lived he on
Till hope and all but agony were gone.

Eight days of pain had passed.   The evening star
Already gleamed in azure depths, afar,
When, like some sea bird vast, a sail drew nigh,
Paused by the pine to hear the victim's cry,
And gentle hands raised to a friendly deck,
The lone surviver of the foundered wreck.

*The steamship Nautilus, belonging to the " Southern
Steamship Company," was wrecked by the hurricane which
swept over the Gulf of Mexico on the 10th of August, 1856,
and by which Last Island was destroyed.   She was at the
time on her way from Galveston to New Orleans with quite
a number of passengers.   All on board perished, with the
exception of the colored steward, Jim Frisby, who was
rescued on the eighth day, as above described.

WONDERS OF NATURE.

ASK you for mystery ?—then look upon
The ever changing miracle of life,
And if you can, trace out the wondrous link
Unseen, which joins the living to the dead.
The dead were living once, ere those, our friends,
Had form and being ; aye, and those whose life
Now charms the eye of animated dust,
Live, on what lived before. The flower of spring
Which gathers fragrance from the foulest spot,
And gives delicious odors to the breeze,
Where was it once ? whence came it ? who can trace
The story of its atoms ?

One little month before
It ope'd its petals to the wooing winds,
Where was the scented incense of its charm ?
Where were those softly-tinted flow'ret-leaves,
O'er which a more than angel skill has left
The traces of its genius ?—canst thou tell ?
Or, with thy " mind's creative eye " discern
Aught half so wonderful ? Oh ! marvel not
" The glorious king of day " bends low to kiss
These " handiworks " which Nature's potent art

Hath wrought out with an alchimistic charm
From Earth's discordant elements.   The dust,
The stagnant and polluted water-pool,
And the revolting triumphs of decay,
Unsav'ry and unsightly, these, aye, these
Are the materialities, with which
Nature performs her wonders.   But e'en here
We find the oft-used elements which have
A thousand times assumed a thousand shapes,
And will a thousand thousand shapes assume
Ere Nature bids them rest.   All other things
Which glory in the plastic life of earth,
Like to the flow'rets, flourish and decay,
Then wake renewed to being.   Thus it is
Through all the fibres of that silver chord
Which circles round existence.   But in man
A stranger mystery, combined, appears—
A mental—moral—mortal mystery !
See'st thou that strange expression in his eye ?
That stirring in his blood ?   His face appears
To bear slight record, in its changeful flush,
Of some internal converse.   Deep within
The vast profundity of noiseless thought
There seems a movement which communicates
A mystic impress to his speaking eye,
The mirror of his soul.
     Even that eye
Now sparkling with so eloquent a sheen,
Will all its lustre lose, if we withhold
The nurture of the body.   And that cheek

Which crimsons o'er with innocence or shame
Will lose the rushing freshness of its blood
If food be but denied.   Does thought, concealed,
And undeveloped, find a lurking place
In each insensate clod which ministers
To give organic growth ?   Is that which leads
To thought its spirit-wing, itself unwinged ?
Is the low produce of the teeming earth,
An atom of the soul ?   Cease, daring thought,
Nor farther tempt the strange inquiry,
Which spurns at thy connection with the dust.

WHAT IS LOVE LIKE?

LIKE the balmy breath of the early spring
   Is the first fond dream of love—
A spirit which sighs on its viewless wing,
   And comes as from worlds above.

Like the voiceless music which breathes delight
   In the mystic and ceaseless roll
Of the starry hosts, that in robes of light,
   Hymn bliss to the raptur'd soul.

Like the Moslem's dream of a happier land,
   When he gives to his fancy wing,
And the courtly charms of a Houri band
   Love's flow'rets around him fling.

Like the sun-born ray which awakes the hues
   Of the blossoms that deck the plain,
And scatters its tints through the morning dews
   Which have mirrored some fairy train.

Like the joyous song of the forest bird,
   As it warbles its blissful láy,
When the leaflet worlds in the winds are stirred,
   And the sylvan nymphs are at play :

Such, such is love—may its blissful dream,
   With its realm of untold delight
Round thy pathway shine, with a joyous beam
   Of affection, forever bright !

   The foregoing lines, written for a lady's album in St. John's, N. F., were in answer to the question which stands as their heading.

THE MOURNER'S WAIL.

"Blessed are they that mourn, for they shall be comforted."

[The following lines were written at the request of Mrs.
S—, a relative of ex-President Fillmore's, and are intended
to convey a faint idea of her feelings when her two sons
were suddenly called away to the spirit-land, in the bloom
of early manhood.]

AND have ye gone, my children, have ye fled,
   In life's warm spring-time, to that silent
      bourn,
Whose cheerless chambers welcome but the dead,
   And, closing once, admit of no return?

'Twas hard to part!—I loved you well, my boys,
   For oh! your lives were strangely linked with
      mine,—
A part they were of my maternal joys,
   And sad it was to watch your son's decline.

Too soon he came, the minister of fate,
   The pale, grim archer of the fleshless hand,
And left me here, lone and disconsolate,
   As she who mourned the loss of Judah's land.

Grief, like a cloud, hung heavy o'er my soul,
    With starless midnight's all-pervading gloom ;
While round me seemed to stalk the demon-ghole,
    Fresh from his revel feastings in the tomb.

The world appeared all sad : e'en hope had veiled
    The cheering brightness of her angel-face ;
And mournfully the sighing breezes wailed,
    Like the lone echoes of some phantom race.

Then came the silent dullness of despair,
    With the strange solace of out-gushing tears,
Which flow in blessedness, as if to bear
    The heart's deep sorrows in their pearly spheres.

And sinful seemed my selfish wail ; but soon
    " A still small voice " low whispered in my ear,
Soft as the song-bird's melodies in June,
    And sweet as freighted with an angel's cheer.

" Death is the door of life "—so spake the voice,
    " The darkened portal to the brighter land
Where earth's poor mourners evermore rejoice,
    With the high hymns of an immortal band.

" Thy sons are living still—a larger life
    Than earth can give, or death can take away,
Is theirs—existence, freed from care and strife,
    And spirit joys, uncumbered by the clay.

" With them all love is purity, and light
   Beams from its Central Source, so soft and
      clear,
That that which darkness was, becomes all bright,
   And blissful homes, ' not made with hands,'
      appear.

" Immortal fruits there ripen for the blest,
   In God's own garden, of unfading bloom ;
And angels welcome still the stranger guest
   Who comes a weary pilgrim from the tomb."

Thus having breathed, the seraph-whisper ceased;
   But Death no more seemed Terror's tyrant
      King—
The usher, rather, to a sacred feast
   Where ransom'd souls celestial music sing.

THE PLEASURES OF PIETY.

LET worldly mirth hymn loud her syren
     song ;
Let passion-pleasures their enchantments spread ;
Let beauty circle round the festive throng,
    With a fond, rapturous, fantastic tread ;
    Let her extend her hand, and we be led
Through the wild mazes of the stirring dance,
    Where young desire shall be all fondly fed
With nectar-sweets : and love's enkindling glance
Shall call up in the soul a most delusive trance :

Yet these are flow'rets which are doomed to fade ;
    The fleeting breath of transitory joy,
All fragrant for a moment, and then, made
    To mingle with the poisons which destroy :
    These are the sweets which, fondly tasted, cloy
The ardent longings of excited sense ;
    And these the burning glances which destroy,
And leave no soft abiding recompense
To soothe the joyless soul's farewell to Innocence.

But in the peaceful ways of pleasantness,
    Which Piety points out as Virtue's road,
Joys, never-fading, ever-truthful, bless
    The fainting pilgrim, bending 'neath his load ;
    Onward he journeys to a lov'd abode,

Forever seen by Faith's far-stretching eye,
   And grateful for the kindnesses bestowed
By Him who fills the circuit of the sky,
He bows with holy trust, and worships the Most
     High.

His is a sacred pleasure—his a trust
   Which nerves the spirit with a fond delight—
A sweetly savor'd balm, which ever must
   The secret soul to extacies invite,
   Buoyant with cheerful prospects which unite
The earthly and the heav'nly, he appears
   With holy visions on his raptur'd sight,
To look beyond this world of care and tears
To where a fadeless land of happiness appears.

And joyous, too, are they—the fair—the young,
   Who folly's cup have never learned to drain ;
Who ne'er have listened to the charmer's tongue,
   Breathing, with skillful lure, the fatal strain ;
   Ne'er have they known the grief-producing pain
Of Thought's compunctious whisper, and im-
     pressed,
   Like the soft calm which, stretching o'er the
     main,
Pictures the deep blue Heav'n in ocean's breast,
They seem to shadow forth the joys of future rest.

VISIT OF THE SUNBEAMS TO THE
FALLS OF NIAGARA.

FROM orient realms, in depths of space afar,
  Young sunbeams travel in their golden car ;
Lightly they glance along old Ocean's breast,
Enkindling sea-gems on each wavelet's crest ;
O'er flow'ry plains and verdant fields they pass,
Where dewy pearls adorn each blade of grass—
Where fragrance rises from the tears of Night
When smiled on by these messengers of light,
These angel visitants of earth, whose ray
Receives its lustre from the God of Day.

Away, away they speed—and many a grove
Sends forth its tuneful melodies to rove
Amid the brightness of their path, and sing
A mournful anthem on exultant wing.
Still on they pass—the cottage and the hall,
The snow-crown'd mount, the ivied castle wall,
The rich man's mansion and the poor man's home
Are lighted by their presence as they roam.

Beside Niagara, entranced, I stood,
Awed by the thunder of its falling flood,
Stilled by the voice of its eternal roar,
Passions were lull'd and fancy taught to soar.

'Twas early morn, and as the Sunbeams came
In golden grandeur from a world of flame,
They reveled in their brightness, mid the trees,
Whose fresh leaves fluttered in the whisp'ring
        breeze,
Then rested, old Niagara, on thee—
Sov'reign of streams and type of majesty!
Thy smiling courtiers, rising from thy feet,
Rise up on wings of amber-mist to greet
Sol's bright ambassadors—they meet—they bring
A rainbow-wreath to crown the Cascade King!
'Twas brightly beautiful! its changeful hues
Were brilliant as the love-dreams of the muse;
While blending glories glittered in each gem
Set in that fair supernal diadem.

On pass thy Sunbeams and the vapors bright
In mystic dance of loveliness and light;
Wildly they wander through the fields of air,
Or stoop to kiss sweet Flora's children fair;
New charms expand in the bright, beauteous race,
And fragrance welcomes still the fond embrace;
With ever-varying tint each petal glows,
The smiling lily hails the blushing rose—
Still on they go, through garden, field and grove,
In ceaseless rounds of harmony and love!

THE SONG OF LABOR.

[Written by request, and read at the Anniversary celebration of the "Screwman's Benevolent Association," of New Orleans.]

HO ! idling drones of this teeming earth,
  Make way for the sons of toil,
Who redeem the promise implied by birth,
  And live not by theft or spoil ;
Faith clings to the manly and honest grasp,
  And brightens their eagle-glance,
And lordlings quake, like the trembling asp,
  As the sons of toil advance.

With a stalwart arm and a trenchant blade
  The forests are cleared away,
And Labor laughs, as with hoe and spade
  It delves in the virgin clay :
Whate'er it touches is turned to gold ;
  Fair fruitful fields appear
Where deserts moaned in the days of old,
  And knew not the harvest's cheer.

There's a magic charm in the toiler's hand—
  An all but creative might—
Which a thought can clothe, and a dream expand,
  Till they burst on the gazer's sight

In temples fair, and in fabrics strange—
  The triumphs of plastic art ;
Which can give to Science its widest range,
  And to Commerce its golden mart.

The stately ship, which in pride careers
  O'er the wilds of the pathless sea,
And the mystic needle by which she steers,
  Brave toiler, were made by thee :
The freight she bears is thy gathered store,
  From mountain and field and mine—
From the forest shade, from the pearl-strewn shore,
  And the caverned depths of brine.

Thou'st built the palace and sacred fane,
  And fashioned the kingly crown :
The cities which smile upon hill and plain,
  And forts to defend or frown ;
The broad canal and the iron rail,
  And the lightning's nerve-like wire,
Which can thrill with thoughts, or in sadness wail,
  Like the strings of Apollo's lyre.

The household gods in the lowly home
  Are sacred made by thee :
They are dear as the perfumed amber-foam
  To the gods of the sounding sea.
The things of use, and for courtly show,
  Spring alike from thy cultured skill :
Then assert thy rights, and let rulers know
  The might of the toiler's will !

Ho ! idling drones of this teeming earth,
   Make way for the sons of toil,
Who redeem the promise implied by birth,
   And live not by theft or spoil :
Faith clings to their manly and honest grasp
   And brightens their eagle-glance,
And lordlings quake like the trembling asp',
   When the sons of toil advance.

HENRY CLAY.

[The following lines, written at the request of the New Orleans "Clay Monument Association," were read by the Author at the laying of the Corner-Stone of the Monument, on Canal-street, April 12th, 1856.]

LONELY the mill-boy wends his weary way,
Too soon inured to toil. A mother's wants—
A widowed mother's—claim his young regard,
And labor is a pleasure. Sometimes thoughts,
Prophetic of the future, stir his soul,
And give ambition wings. Golden and grand
The hills of Fame, in the dim distance, rise
All spangled o'er with triumphs, and he feels
That he can mount them with an earnest tread,
And wreathe a fadeless chaplet for his brow.

Nature is his instructor :—trees and flowers ;
The sparkling gems in Night's cerulean dome ;
The spring-time warblers, and th' insensate clod—
All teach him wondrous lore. Bright as the sheen
Of an archangel's wing his thoughts take form
In rudimental beauty, but his tongue,
As yet unskilled in verbal witcheries,
All vainly strives to give them fitting speech.

Time speeds its flight : the mill-boy's hopes expand,
Friends gather round with kindly proffered aid,
And he becomes a student.   Books are his—
The treasure-tomes of deep forensic skill—
Mazes of written and unwritten law—
And he attempts the hard though pleasant task
Of searching out their hidden mysteries.

Who speaks of failure to that ardent boy ?
He scorns the timid word !   His soul has grown
On young ambition's manna, and he dreams
That he shall yet so fix his name on Time
That all the Future cannot blot it out.
And oh ! his mother mingles with his dream ;
That gentle mother, who, in poverty,
Had trained his infant steps ; and in his eyes
Had looked her doting love ; and in his ear
Had breathed a mother's purest, kindest thoughts.
And so, the boy dreams on, and studies on—
Each day a new success !   The richest stores
Of legal erudition soon are his,
And with the strength of a fresh giant mind
He boldly joins in the polemic fray.

Now, like "the star of empire," westernward
He onward speeds, and where Kentucky's fields
Spread out its virgin beauty, he begins
The summer labors of an active life.

With "the stern joy" the generous foeman feels,
When battling with the brave, in mental strife

He meets the ablest jurists of the West,
Reason his sword, and eloquence his shield.
Strong as the heaving of a mountain wave ;
Playful as zephyrs toying with fair flowers ;
Clear as the light, and luminous as stars,
His thoughts take wing, and clothe themselves
 with words.

In proud preëminence, high over all,
Like Saul above his fellows, forth he stands,
A giant among giants. Soon the halls
Of legislation echo to his voice,
While plaudits hail the wisdom of his speech.
Deep, vast and comprehensive, now his mind
In questions of high polity engaged,
Becomes a nation's guide.

   When storms arise
His are the clarion-tones which counsel war,
While others prate of "Peace!" Honor and
 Right !
The flag's protective pow'r !—these are his themes;
And when, with burning words, he gives them
 voice,
The pulses of a people's will are stirr'd,
As fierce winds stir the ocean to its depths.
His counsels sage time fails not to approve :
The seas gain other sov'reigns ; and the name
Of proud Columbia brightens to a world—
The dread of despots, but *the hope of man !*

With the charm'd utterance of " Compromise,"
He breathes a spell, and civil discord ends ;
Strife shrinks within its covert, exorcised,
And the broad Union hails the cherish'd word !
He, too, is Freedom's pleader—he, the wise,
The brave, the eloquent, the nation's guide !
He pleads for struggling Greece ; and every sound
Is turned into a sword.   But for his voice,
The noblest river of this Western land—
Our own broad Mississippi—would have been
The claim of rival powers, and the source
Of fierce contention and of wasting wars.

So lived he on—the statesman and the sage :—
And when the herald from the shining land
Appeared to claim him, firm at duty's post
The Christian Tribune pleading still was found—
Pleading for Brotherhood and Compromise !

He passed !—from breathing dust to endless life—
From earth's closed labors to supernal spheres !

Gone is the peerless commoner, self-made,
Whose acts were all a triumph ; who, to gain
The proudest honors in a nation's gift,
Would ne'er forsake the right ; and now, his praise
Falls from all lips in heartfelt gratitude.
Fitting it is his cenotaph to rear
In view of the glad waters of that tide

Whose Commerce speaks his constant eulogy :
This is the corner-stone : and here to-day
Assembled thousands see it firmly laid.
Above, to bear his fame to latest time,
In monumental marble, shall arise
The faint translation of a grateful thought
Which swells in each true breast for HENRY CLAY.

LIGHT.

Light, beautiful light !
Light, the reflection of Deity's smile,
That wakeneth worlds from the chaos of night,
　And brighteneth ocean and isle.
Fleet as a thought o'er the waters careering,
Iris hued pearls in thy pathway appearing,
Gleam on the foam, while the depths thou art
　　cheering—
　　　　Light, beautiful light !

Light, cherishing light !
Light as it lingers o'er forest and field—
That tinteth the flowers to gladden the sight,
　And brightens their emerald shield.
Thou to the gardens, in glory descending,
Mystical beauties forever art blending,
While to the fruit-trees rich treasures thou'rt
　　lending—
　　　　Light, cherishing light !

Light, gladdening light !
Light that converteth to diamonds the dew,
That wakens the morn with a hymn of delight,
　As if 'twere created anew !

When over nature thy mantle thou'rt flinging,
Groves become vocal, and birds with their singing
Gush forth in praise, like a fountain upspringing—
        Light, gladdening light !

        Light, truth-telling light !
    Light as it comes from the radiant spheres,
That shadows dispels with its silvery might,
    And dangers and phantoms and fears.
Bright through the lattice thy matin rays streaming,
Startle the maid from her passionate dreaming,
Showing the true from that only in seeming—
        Light, truth-telling light !

        Light, heavenly light !
    Light, as in brightness it beams on the mind,
That seems with a pencil of glory to write
    High lyrics of hope for mankind.
Mortals, the mystical tablet divining,
Still for the fair and the holy are pining,
While their best thoughts thou art upwards
        inclining—
        Light, heavenly light !

KEEP STEP TO THE MUSIC.

"Keeping step to the music of the Union."—RUFUS CHOATE.

KEEP step to the music—the music that
    thrills
The national heart, from the sea to the hills,
And which in one glorious anthem combines
Its holiest hopes and its noblest designs.

Keep step to the music—though traitors advance
With a banner of black, and with uplifted lance,
Be our footfall but firm they will soon pass away,
Like the dew-damps of night in the brightness
    of day !

Keep step to the music—that song of the stars
Which brighten our standard—come peace or
    come wars.
Our step shall be true, and THE UNION shall be
The watchword and hope of the brave and the
    free !

Keep step to the music—and trample in scorn
On fratricide foemen of treachery born;
Tear down their black banner, and raise in its
stead
The flag 'neath which freemen and heroes can
tread.

Keep step to the music—its tones are as dear
As the voices of home, to the patriot's ear :
The march is a Nation's, whose States e'er
shall be,
" Distinct as the billows, yet one as the sea."

The above lines were written in 1856, and were set to
music by M. THEODORE VON LA HACHE, of New Orleans.

·   LINES.

[Written for a Lady's "Hair Album," at Niagara.]

DEAR braided locks ! which tell
    Of the distant, the departed,
As the songs of ocean murmur in the shell ;
    And which whisper—" All is well !"
    When we might be lonely hearted
And with voiceless music mystically swell.

    Locks fair, and dark, and gray,
    Erst to kindred ringlets mated ;
Severed from the crowns of loved ones now away.
    Some in spirit-gardens stray,
    Warmed by suns all uncreated,
And some still linger with us in the clay.

    To other times ye pass,
    Bright aids to recollection,
Mirroring the storied past as in a glass,
    And shall we cry, alas !
    In our spirit's deep dejection,
For those cut down and withered as the grass ?

No : they shall reappear
In a land of light unending,
Where no eye shall e'er be dimmed by a tear—
In that higher, purer sphere
Where celestial glories blending,
Shall form a crown for those who triumph here.

THE DREAM OF THE FIRST INFANT.

IN days of bliss when the earth was young,
  And the flow'rets laughed in their primal birth,
When song-birds fluttered the groves among,
  And 'wakened the echoes of sinless mirth ;
Then, then was the pride of the garden given—
The choicest gift of indulgent heaven—
And man was glad ; for a richer sheen
Seemed born with the smile of his Eden-queen.

With gayer plumage and sweeter voice,
With purer fragrance and tints more choice,
The birds and flowers appeared to bring
To the bridal bower their offering.
So rich and rare was that bridal gift,—
  So pure and dulcet the spousal song,
That they seemed the souls of the lov'd to lift
  To the courts of bliss where the angels throng.

*   *   *   *   *

On a sunny morn of another spring,
When the birds of Eden were gay of wing,
When the sunbeams danced and the playful breeze
With the green leaves toyed of the incense-trees,
As sporting mid treasures of opening bloom,
Its pinions were laden with rich perfume ;
On that sunny morn, where a gentle stream
Was kissed by the light's most golden beam,
Beneath the shade of that fabled tree,
Whose leaves were attuned to minstrelsy,
A mother sat—'twas a thing of joy,
To see her there with her first-born boy—
That first fond mother—for pure and fair
They seemed as they sat together there.

Oh, bright was the smile on that mother's face
    As the wing of the angel that passed her by,
When her glances of love first learned to trace
    The picture of thought in her infant's eye.
The wings of the angel might yet be seen,
And the sceptre he bore, with its dazzling sheen,
And his beautiful face half hidden from sight
In a graceful halo of heavenly light ;
And never before had that earth-born child
    Looked out on a picture which seemed so fair,
And the earliest mother of infants smiled,
    As if in the joy of her child to share.

'Twas a morn of beauty—the birds so gay,
With gorgeous plumage, from spray to spray,

All lightly moved, and their melody   .
Seemed to echo the tones of the minstrel-tree.
The blossoms, the buds and the emerald shade,
The pearly stream where the sunbeams played,
The light and the song, and zephyr's flight
Gave birth to the transports of young delight.
O, ne'er was the spirit of infancy
    Awakened to thought in a scene more blessed,
And never was child on its mother's knee
    More dearly loved, or more fondly pressed.

      *   *   *   *   *

As calm as the petals which gently close
When the eve invites them to soft repose,
And pure as the dew which from heaven fall·
When the stars illumine their azure halls,
So calm and pure did refreshing sleep
O'er that infant's senses its vigils keep.

The mother whispered a lullaby,
    To deepen the sleep of the slumberer,
And the voice of the angel gave sweet reply,
    In tones of delight that were new to her ;
Then the angel plumed his wings for flight,
    As a guide to that infant's spirit thought ;
And wondrous visions of beauty and light
    To the ken of the dreamer were swiftly brought.

In dreams through many a beauteous land,
The infant and angel went hand in hand,
And mountain and forest, and flood and shore,
And rivers which sparkled with golden ore,
And wonders of sea, and of earth and sky,
Seemed pictured in light to that infant's eye.

Then away through the boundless blue, afar,
Where kindles the beam of the farthest star ;
Beyond the reach of the tinted ray
Which limits the realm of the sun-god's day,
Away, away, seemed the wanderer's flight,
Till the gates of heaven appeared in sight.

" Open the gates," did the angel cry,
    " I come with a spirit that's free from sin ;"
And a silv'ry voice said in kind reply,
    " The pure and spotless can enter in."

The gates were opened—the seraphs smiled
On that lovely angel-directed child,
But the highest spirit could scarce declare,
The countless glories that centered there.
No more to that child seemed the gems of earth
Of peerless beauty, and priceless worth,
And the sea-born pearls and the stars of even
Seemed dust when compared with the gems of
        heaven.

" Such," said the angel, " thy lot shall be—
    These visions of glory shall e'er remain,
If thy spirit in infant purity
    Be kept from error's polluting stain.

The child awoke ; and its mother's eye
    Was bright with a lustrous and grateful gleam,
For she knew that the angel that then stood by
    Had guided the course of her infant's dream.

ODE TO SPRING.

HAIL to thee, SPRING!
Again thou comest with thy chosen sweets;
Again our cheeks thy perfumed breathing greets;
    While birds, on wing,
Tinted with iris-hues, from every tree
Are hymning choral welcomes unto thee.

    Where hast thou been,
With all thy fairy ornature of green,
Of sunbeams woven by a hand unseen?—
    Gathering in
The life-seed of some precious floral gem
To decorate thy queenly diadem?

    Or, haply, thou
Hast been a wanderer in other lands,
To cheer up those whom despot Might commands,
    And teach them how
To gather flow'rets from that sacred tree
Which gods and men have christened "LIBERTY!"

If that be so,
Let blessings on thy holy mission rest,
And Freedom's spring-time hopes, within each
breast
Be made to grow,
As grows the bud which clasps the promised
flower,
Beneath the silent magic of thy power.

Long does it seem
Since thou wast here before in all thy charms,
But, welcome now, as to a lover's arms, .
If thou canst deem
The worship of a spirit such as mine,
Worthy of aught like unto thee, divine !

Familiar, now,
Let us hold converse of thy blissful life,
With teeming poesy so sweetly rife,
And for thy brow,
Of thine own flowers, if thou'lt grant me leave,
A simple chaplet I will strive to weave.

Forgive the thought !
No bard of earth can e'er expect to bring
To such as thou a welcome offering,
For, heaven-taught,
The birds to thee sing far diviner lays,
While every leaf has lyrics in thy praise.

Each petal tells,
With all the fragrant eloquence of Truth,
The story of thy never-fading youth ;
    While fairy bells
Open their honied lips to hymn thy fame
In words too pure for human tongues to name.

    Circling around
The changeful surface of God's footstool—Earth,
Thou giv'st the glories of the garden birth ;
    And o'er the ground,
In lowly dale and by the mountain stream,
Are flung thy gifts—pure as an angel's dream.

    No scorching sun
Of summer ever burns upon thy brow,
For thou 'rt away ere Summer comes, and thou,
    Perennial* one !
Canst ne'er know Autumn's " sere and yellow leaf,"
Or Winter's wailing monody of grief.

    I knew a maid,
Fair, almost, as thou art, who used to cull
The blossoms from thy bowers at evening's lull,
    That-she might braid

* The critic may, perhaps, object to the term " Perennial,"
in this connection. The writer's defence is, that Spring—
the personified Spring of Poesy—is ever-existent; passing
from land to land, she has always flowers beneath her feet
and perfume in her breath, and in our own "Sunny South"
she may be said continually to linger.

Of them, a wreath, to deck her virgin brow—
'Tis scarce a year ago—*where is she now?*

      In dreamless sleep !—
A cheerless chamber in the silent tomb !
Corruption's chosen at the feast of Doom !
      Well may we weep,
When that stern robber, Death, in wasteful glee,
Can lay his fleshless hand on such as she.

      But thou, fair Spring,
Art still the same ; as beautiful and young
As when, in Eden's bowers, thy praise was sung,
      On angel's wing,
And thy fresh floral gifts were primal blown
Ere on Temptation's tree the fruit had grown.

      O ! welcome, then,
Thrice welcome, with thy zephyr breath of balm,
Thy bud and blossom, and thy branch of palm ;
      And when again
Thou leav'st us in thy gay and glad career,
Bid our hopes follow round thy floral year.

LINES.

[Written on the death of an aged lady of Boston, England, whose last words were—*"All is well."*]

SHE lay in suffering—the crimson tide
　　With feeble impulse, sought its 'customed
　　　　flow;
But those who loved her still, were by her side,
　　With ready hand, determined to bestow
Whate'er might ease a pang, or be supplied,
　　To sweeten that deep cup, which all below
Must drink, to sorrows past, before they stand
'Mid the green fields of the celestial land.

And willingly she drank;—her fourscore years
　　Had taken, of that bitter cup, away
Much of its bitterness; for pains and tears
　　Had made the silver chord of life decay
With gradual infirmity.　No fears,
　　Urged her to wish her spirit's longer stay
In that frail tenement, so long the load
Which kept it from its heaven-gem'd abode.

And " all is well," she said, with latest breath,
    And, ALL IS WELL !—how sweetly does the sound
Come, angel voic'd—a harbinger of death—
    From those to the unfading Eden bound !
It speaks immortal trust,—and of that wreath
    Where Faith and Hope, in sweet embrace are
        found
Joined to that pure and everlasting Vine,
Planted by Love, where suns eternal shine.

FAREWELL.

FAREWELL ! O sad and tender word,
   How deep thy magic spell !
For friends, in cot or gilded hall,
   'Tis hard to say—Farewell !

Farewell—it lingers on the tongue,
   While many a pleasing dream
Calls up, anew, long-past delights
   From life's uneven stream.

Farewell—what pen can e'er record—
   What tongue can ever tell,
The burning thoughts which cluster round
   That magic word—FAREWELL !

THE FORSAKEN ONE.*

SHE grew in loveliness, a fair young thing,
   O'er which the angels seemed their smiles
       to fling
In rich profusion ; and as gentle, she,
As the light breeze which wafts from Eden's tree
Undying odors through the breathing air,
To bless and circulate forever there.
And as she grew in loveliness, her thought,
By Fancy's bright ideal teachings taught,
Pictured a thousand scenes of untold bliss
And peopled all with dreams of happiness.

---

* " THE FORSAKEN ONE " is no imaginary character. The writer became acquainted with her melancholy history while standing beside her grave in Newfoundland, where she lived, and loved, and died! She is said to have been remarkably beautiful and intellectual, and her memory will long be sacredly cherished by the fair daughters of Terra Nova. The reason why she was so heartlessly forsaken, and but a few days before that appointed for her marriage, arose from sectarian prejudices fostered in the mind of her lover by his friends. The lines, as above, were hastily written on ship-board, and an imperfect copy of them has already appeared in print.

Her heart was like a harp, wooed by the winds,
And, grateful for the music which it finds
Trill from its strings in sweetest melody,
Asks not the wooers if they ere shall flee.
She loved her relatives, her friends, and all
The flowers that bloom at Spring's omnific call ;
She loved the birds, the wilds, the purple sea,
The stars which light up heaven's immensity,
The regal splendor of the mid-day sun,
And the rich glories, when his course is run,
Which gild the curtains of the glowing West,
To decorate his couch of rosy rest.

But one there was, who ever used to seem,
In the fond trustings of young passion's dream,
Brighter and fairer, aye, and fonder too,
Than all beside that ever met her view ;
His many faults all others could descry,
Yet faultless still he stood before her eye
As angels are, that breathe in courts above,
An atmosphere of worship and of love.
Though every friend opposed, she loved him yet,
And still believed he never could forget
The vows and promises so oft-times made
In that fair bower, in whose spangled shade
They've sat, time after time, as eve stole on,
And watched " Night's silvery queen " ascend her
    throne,
With all the star-nymphs that attend her train,
To sing the wonders of the blissful reign.

Thus have they sat, the loving and the loved,
And if a zephyr in that arbor moved
One em'rald gem, one flower supporting leaf,
She'd count it an intruder, and a thief,
That came to rob her ear, she knew not why,
Of its fond treasure—her own loved one's sigh.

But time passed on, and he, the loved, became
Careless of her, her off'rings and her flame.
The treasures of her love were prized no more ;
He fled ! and all her happiness was o'er,
Save when in prayer she sought heaven's blissful
     shade,
And prayed that choicest blessings might be
     made
To hover, like a dream of light, above
The future footsteps of her faithless love.

'Twas winter, and the frost-king reared his
     throne
Where meteor lights illumed his frozen zone,
While his chill palace, of the water-rock,
Braved the rude tempest and the storm-waves
     shock.
Cold as the breathings of his cheerless court,
Where pleasure never wreathed the smiles of
     sport,
Were all the smiles of all the world to her
Who would her faithless love to all prefer.

Spring came with birds and flowers : she fain
  would take
One ramble more around that star-gemmed lake
Where oft with him she'd roved in hours of joy,
Ere blighted hopes were missioned to destroy.
But, ah ! she could not, for in health's decay,
A frost had touched the blossoms of her May.
The roses on her cheek were seen to fade ;
The fond confidings of that trusting maid,
So cruelly deceived, could ne'er again
Picture a scene that was not full of pain.
Birds sang, and flow'rets bloomed, but could not
  bring
The virgin freshness of love's early spring.
To her young mind the bloom of hope was
  past,
And withered, as if touched by that death-blast
Which o'er the burning desert speeds its way,
To scatter desolation and decay.
Day after day witnessed her health's decline ;
Though beauty lingered round its cherished
  shrine,
And yet continued, when with dying breath
She welcomed on the stern approach of death !
The spoiler grim, beheld with envious view
The little love had left him there to do,
And when, at length, he threw his fated dart,
A ray of pity touched his bloodless heart,
To see her so resigned, so meek, so fair,—
To hear the breathings of her latest prayer,

For when the lamp of life was waxing dim,
Forgetful of herself, she prayed for him,
And *dead to all beside*, she still was heard,
Breathing his name—a fond and fatal word !

THE JOURNEY OF A SIGH.

A SIGH ! a woman's sigh of love,
　　Was borne on a zephyr's wing ;
To the bright and beauteous courts above,
　　Where unfading flow'rets spring.

An angel met that love-fraught sigh,
　　As it roamed on its pinions bright ;
With a smile of promise, he asked it—" why
　　It had entered the land of light ?"

" I come," its peerless spirit said,
　　" As the whisper of love's young dream ;
From my earthly home I have fondly fled
　　To where lights celestial gleam :

And pure is the tale of love I bear,
　　As the sheen of thine own bright wing ;
For the love is pure, and the lady fair,
　　Whose whispers of soul I bring.

For her I ask all the joys of earth,
　　And a place 'mid the blest, in Heaven ;"
And the angel said—" To the child of worth,
　　Both, both shall be freely given."

A VISION.

"I had a dream which was not all a dream."—BYRON.

'TWAS in the hush of midnight—Sorrow's wail
    Died on my ear, as sleep its mystic veil
Threw o'er my senses, and my unchain'd soul,
Freed from terrestrial bondage and control,
Panted for fearless flight. Fancy stood by,
With wild adventurous daring in her eye ;
" Dost wish," said she, " to course, on burnish'd
    wing,
The perfumed regions of unending spring ?
To triumph over space—from star to star,
To roll, majestic, in my viewless car ?
To raise the spirits of the earth and air—
The stern, the dismal, or the bright and fair ?
Or trace the Future, with its flux of years,
Its strifes, its triumphs, and ·its smiles and
    tears ?
Or wilt thou course with me Time's ether track,
On his own wings to trace his pathway back,
And view the wondrous Past—its dying throes,
Its short-lived pleasures, and its ceaseless woes ?"

"I'd see the Past," I said; "with strange
    delight,
I'd view the spot where Time commenced his
    flight ;
I'd sweep the spell of centuries away—
Catch the first beam which lit the god of day—
List the first hymn the forest warblers sung—
Trace up the path of Time since Time was
    young—
His every record read, till he shall be
Lost in the cycles of Eternity."
    This said, hours, days, weeks, months and years
    unroll
The register of Time's swift-written scroll ;
Ages speed back in retrograding flight—
The Past becomes the Present—thickest night
Hangs round in sable gloom :—I stood before
Time's birth, Day's morn, or Ocean's first hoarse
    roar.
    A voice is heard, omnific in its might—
"LET THERE BE LIGHT !" it said—and *all was light !*
Earth's beauties, sparkling, kiss the heaven-born
    rays,
And stars and angel-bands chant songs of praise :
Through the dark clouds of chaos quickly shine
Creation—order—harmony—design !
Life and her teeming millions stand displayed—
A week is ended, and a world is made !
    But here one spot appears most purely bright—
The home of love—the garden of delight :

Sweet birth-place of Humanity !—is this
The scene which fostered earliest dreams of bliss ?—
The scene where Earth her first fair off'rings
    spread ?
Where man, delighted, on her bounties fed ?
Aye, 'tis !—and Innocence here found a grave—
Here Disobedience rolled its first fell wave—
Hate, Malice, Strife and Envy here were born,
And here first grew the bramble and the thorn.

    Time passes onward—man extends his race—
Earth marks her orbit through her wilds of space ;
The millions plod in rounds of vice and pride,
On plain and valley, hill and mountain side ;
Their thousand wants the teeming earth supplies ;
In thanklessness they grasp the varied prize,
Then mock Omnipotence—His power deride,—
His deluge comes—they sink beneath its tide !

    One dying groan with horror fills my ears !
One ocean-vested plain the earth appears,
And 'neath that plain is hid full many a cave,
Where Art and Nature find one common grave.
Dark Desolation reigns : I look—Affright
Spreads tracts of waste before my wand'ring
    sight—
Of watery waste—a wide, wild liquid robe—
The grave of crime—the vestment of a globe !

    One barque, the safe retreat of life and rest,
A world of waters bears upon its breast ;
Alone she triumphs o'er th' aquatic tomb,
A world's inhabitants within her womb,—

A future world—o'er which Heaven's bow of love,
In lines of mercy smiles from depths above.
   Th' avenging wave recedes: Earth's plains again
Are peopled by the toiling sons of men ;
Age after age arrays its flight of years—
Man's every act upon their page appears,
And crime, and pain, and misery's increase,
Are found to blend with virtue, love and peace.
   Now deeds, unwritten, catch my watchful eye,
But Time advances, and I pass them by :
War hurls its thunders ; Earth's broad field
    appears
One moving forest of contending spears,—
Death cheers his angels loud with groan and yell :
But stop I not the story dire to tell,
Of him who conquered, or who fell below
The tiger-vengeance of the foeman's blow ;
For War but feebly treads the walks of death,
Compared with him who fans his poison breath :
Let War array in all the pomp of pride,
His giant-angels by thy horrent side,
INTEMPERANCE, and pigmies they become—
Their every tongue, compared with thine, is dumb.
   Now Fancy waves her hand before my sight ;
Earth disappears ;—a region richly bright,
Superlatively lovely, grand and fair,
From heaven's four corners spans the depths of
    air :
All that can charm the eye of man, or please
His sense, or yield him happiness or ease,

Are here profusely scattered : Fragrance brings
Perfume upon the zephyr's playful wings,
From many a spicy grove, whose leaflets sport
Where feathery minstrels hold their choral court ;
And o'er its fertile surface, rivers glide,
And milk and honey swell their silv'ry tide,
And on their banks unnumber'd flow'rets blow,
Their beauties mirror'd on the streams below.
   " O lovely spot !" my spirit inly cried ;
" Such might be earth !" *a still, small voice* re-
     plied ;
And as it spoke, a bright terrestrial train
Of men like angels course th' Elysian plain.
   " See'st thou yon cloud ?" said Fancy, and mine
     eye
Sought a dark spot which marked the Eastern sky :
It grew, and spread its gloomy wings of night,
Which might the shades of Erebus affright,
Until its woe-inspiring shadows fell
On that bright land, and, wonderful to tell,—
Where the dark shadow threw its blackest stain,
A fiery river coursed the fertile plain.
Dark Desolation marked it, for it drew
The only sweets from every plant that grew,
And turned them into poison ; and its fumes
Rose on the winds, and revel'd 'mong the tombs.
Man breathed the sickly odors, and a vain
And wild infatuation filled his brain :
He steeped his senses in the burning flood,
Then madly cried for vengeance and for blood.

As 'mong the plants, the sweetest most com-
bined
To swell the demon stream—among mankind,
The bright, the noble, and the gen'rous most
Were lured to join the sense-drown'd victim host:
And first the social were induced to brave
The wild, enchanting, life-destroying wave.

Methinks I see the suff'ring thousands now,
With haggard cheek, and wildly pallid brow,
Whose trembling reason scarcely can abide
The horrid stenches of the Stygian tide :
Methinks I see them struggling 'gainst the force
Which sweeps them onward, in its headlong
course,
To gulfs of darkest night—while some appear
To moan their fate with many a scalding tear ;
On these, Delirium breathes, and, night and day,
Infuriate demons round their senses play ;
Discord unutterable fills their ears,
And laughing goblins mock them with their jeers.
Of those, deep draughts with fury fill the brain,
And loose the bands which hold Destruction's rein,
To madly weave the blood-bespotted wreath
Of direful Murder with the fangs of death !
See trembling millions tread the margin's brink—
Timid they stoop, one dang'rous draught to drink:
Habit on taste its trembling tie makes fast—
The conscience-guarded Rubicon is past ;
Tie after tie destroys each power to save,
And prematurely ope's the insatiate's grave !

O Vault of Terror—shrine of Terror's king !—
The drunkard's grave ! Could I the tear-drops
    bring,
Drawn from Affection's eye by thy chill fear,
A woe-charged flood of sorrows would appear !
Or could I list the orphan's cheerless cry,
And deep-toned anguish of the widow's sigh,
Which thou hast known, O, then would Earth
    unstore,
From the deep treasures of its storied lore,
Its darkest tale of grief, whose words would rise,
To wake the moaning echoes of the skies,
While stories dire of crime and pain would be
Roused from their slumbers in the mighty sea !
    Now, where that cloud of darkness first was seen,
A star of glory rose, whose peerless sheen
Smiled with an angel sweetness o'er the plain
Where drunkenness had fixed its deadly stain,
And rolled along its desolating wave,
The earth to poison and her sons enslave.
And as that star in brightness rose, its light
Dispelled the cloud which hung round Error's night;
Dried up the stream of Death, whose poison tide
The cups of sorrow, and of crime supplied ;
And left that land, in comfort's smiling glow,
With verdure crowned, and milk and honey's flow.
Its storms of strife were lulled ; and Peace arose
In angel triumphs o'er her prostrate foes,
And sweet domestic bliss assumed her reign,
And Love and Joy awoke in smiles again.

I looked—and Fancy's wand again was reared
And all her bright creation disappeared ;
That land was lost—its purifying star
No longer shone from ether wilds, afar—
All, all was changed ; and strange that change
    did seem,
As vision-painted worlds in childhood's dream.
  " That land," said Fancy, "just to chaos hurled,
Prophetic, speaks the changes of a world ;
Like it, this world was lovely once, and fair,—
Like it, 'twas fostered with an angel's care,—
Like it, its brightness faded, and its charm
Was lost for vice, for madness and alarm ;
And like it, too, 'twill change once more, and then
Love's lights will brighten in the homes of men,
And linger, dream-like, round the hallow'd spot
Of quiet joy, and soul-delighting thought !
Blest be that change! unmixed with grief and guile;
And blest the rainbow promise of its smile,
Which, Like the iris, with its changeful dye,
Bends from the earth, and centres in the sky !
Blest be that harbinger of happier years !
That ark of safety o'er a sea of tears !
Where Happiness enjoys a calm retreat,
When Sorrow's surges round her madly beat."
  Again I looked :—before my anxious eye,
The circling flight of years swept swiftly by ;
Earth and earth's scenes rolled on their changeful
    round,
And busy life gave forth its ceaseless sound.

War and Ambition barter'd human blood !
And *Human Honor* drank the purple flood !
Wing'd Commerce triumph'd o'er the briny seas,
And wrote her mottoes on the viewless breeze ;
Faction contended in the courts of strife,
And Schism spurned the laws of holy life :
Still, to each ill, INTEMP'RANCE gave its store,
And made all evils greater than before.

　　And thus it was till TEMPERANCE arose,
In panoply of brightness, o'er the foes
Of life's enjoyment, and her woeless chain
Of sympathy embraced each child of pain.
She rose in loveliness, a seraph-smile
Around her looks of kindness played the while :
Her victories were friendly, and her hand,
Strewed blessings freely o'er each conquer'd land,
And gave that bliss she could alone bestow,—
A bliss Debauch and Crime can never know.

　　Still Time moves onward, and anon appears,
In vision bright, the roll of future years :
Earth in her age grew glorious to my sight,
In the clear lustre of Millennial light ;
And O ! 'twas joy her radiant form to trace !
A beauteous Island in the sea of space,
O'er which a world of bloom profusely springs,
To deck a footstool for the King of kings !

　　But not alone the flowery plain appears,
In hues still brighter than in by-gone years ;
Blending, in loveliness, terrestrial dyes
With colors, uncreated, from the skies ;

A bloom of mind—a moral bloom is seen,
Which smiles, on earth, with more than earthly
    sheen,
And gives a joy to man unknown before,
Scented with odors from a holier shore ;
Minds now expanded, breathe the foretaste given
Of sweetest fragrance from the fields of heaven ;
And with new tongues of seraph-power they raise
The loudest notes of thankfulness and praise.
    O blest Devotion ! now art thou divine !
Circled with gems which must forever shine ;
Swelling the notes of harmony and love,
Which rise like incense to the throne above.
And man, the creature of the dust, is blest—
Bliss, unalloyed, is kindled in his breast ;
And Peace, on dove-like pinions, hovers round—
For Strife, with all his demon-wiles, is bound,
That Innocence o'er man her robe may fling,
As pure and spotless as an angel's wing.
Dazzled with brightness, now my eye grew dim,
As Earth reflected back the lights of Him,
The First, the Last, the Midst, and Without
    End !
Whose glories with his works forever blend.
Faint was my view till the last angel came,
And Earth was rolled up as a scroll of flame ;
Time yielded up his pinions with his breath,
And Victory rose triumphant over Death—
A holy pioneer, to pave the way
To the bright gates of uncreated day !

As time gave up his wings, my dream was o'er ;
But ere 'twas done, a fair celestial shore,
In more than Eden-loveliness appeared,
On which a holy cenotaph was reared,
The work of angel bands, who joyed to raise
An ever-during monument of praise
" To TEMPERANCE,"—for so the record ran,—
" *The Child of Virtue, and the Friend of Man!*"
 And now, the spell which bound my senses
  broke—
Earth seemed herself again, and I awoke.

SONG OF THE NEW YEAR.

[January 1st, 1851.]

AWAY have the days of another year
　　By the angel of Time been cast,
To record the tale of their fleet career,
　　'Mid the depths of the changeless Past.
And away, away, as the moments sped,
　　Full many a hope and fear
Were buried in dust 'neath the death-fiend's
　　tread,
　　Ere the birth of the new-born year.

But not alone in the march of Time,
　　As he measured his ceaseless round,
Were the death of hope and the growth of crime,
　　And the spear of the spoiler found :
For joy was the gift of the gay old year,
　　When his days into season's grew,
And the flowers of Spring and the harvest's cheer
　　Did his garland and crown renew.

And joy was his when the laughing hours
  Were breathing of Love's perfume,
As they lingered in bliss mid the roseate bowers,
  Which Affection's lights illume ;
And joy was his, as he chased away
  Disease from the fevered brain,
And gave, in exchange, life's wonted play,
  For the gnawing tooth of pain.

But mixed and strange is the tale of Time,
  As he telleth it, page by page,
Melodious now, in mused rhyme,
  And fearful now with rage :
Sometimes his words are soft and sweet
  As the Zephyr's fragrant breath,
And sometimes thunder-toned—and meet
  To tell of thy triumphs, Death.

Now does he visit the Congress hall,
  With a look all staid and wise,
And tracing his cyphers along the wall,
  He frameth the " Compromise"—
And forth he sendeth it far and wide,
  And sweareth by yea and nay,
That by it the North and the South shall abide,
  And the UNION shall last for aye.

But not on Senates alone looks Time,
  For he circles the ends of earth,
From the Arctic wilds to the burning clime,
  Where the Alchemist's dream hath birth ;

He looks on the delver's toil-marked hands,
    As by Sacramento's wave
They are plied full well, mid the glittering sands
    To dig out a golden grave.

Again he looks on a martial band ;
    And the fiery sons of Mars
Are away o'er the deep ; for their chiefs have
      planned
    That the spangled Banner of Stars
Shall invite to its folds, with shot and song,
    The " Gem of the Antilles,"
While Freedom's voice shall the shout prolong
    In the swell of the Carib seas.

Another sound !—and the gay old Time
    Half ceaseth his onward march ;
For melodious whispers, which seem divine,
    Ascend on a heavenly arch
To greet his ear with a blissful strain
    Of *mercy and melody*—
A blessed, beautiful, angel twain,
    By the "Swedish bird" set free.

      *   *   *   *   *   *
      *   *   *   *   *   *

IMPROMPTU.

[Written on the banks of the Ohio when a financial panic
was agitating the whole country.]

I STOOD upon a river's bank,
   Beneath the white-armed pride
Of ladies? no—of lofty sycamores ;
And as I stood upon that bank in lonely grief, I
   cried,
A laughing echo to my lay, " *the bank has broke* "
   replied,
   " And fortune has locked up her golden doors."

I REMEMBER THEE.

TO ———

WHEN the morning sun, with a silver tread,
Ascends in the East from his ocean-bed,
When light and joy from the presence spring
Of that mystic orb, which Creation's King
Has placed in his hall of clouds to sway
The seasons of earth with supernal ray,
And sunshine smiles on the land and sea,
Then, then, O then, I remember thee !

When the midday comes, and the noontide beam,
Plays in joyous glee over wave and stream,
And the lowly vale and the mountain glade
Are in vestments of love and of light arrayed ;
Then, then, 'mid the glory of midday sheen,
In the true and the beautiful thou art seen ;
When I look on the fair, and the pure and free,
O then, O then, I remember thee !

When the eve appears and the daylight hies
To his rosy couch in the Western skies,
And the starry gems in " the blue " are seen,
As the jewel'd path of Night's silv'ry queen,

O then, when the song of the grove is still,
And the music alone of the trickling rill
Is heard as it steals through the quiet lea,
I remember thee, I remember thee !

When the visions of night burst on my brain
With the wild delights of a fairy train ;
When an eye which can make my soul rejoice,
And the melting tones of a seraph voice
Are seen and heard, and so much like thine,
That a phantom form, like to thee, divine,
Appears, an angel of purity,
To claim them, then, I remember thee !

LINES.

[To the memory of the Rev. D. A. Fraser, A. M., who died
at St. John's, Newfoundland, in February, 1845.]

HE'S passed away to where " the weary rest,"
The frozen clod lies coldly o'er his breast;
Vacant is now the place he once supplied,
As husband, father, pastor, friend and guide.

He's passed away—the sacred desk no more
Shall echo to his teachings as before ;
No more he'll train for heaven's bright courts above,
His weeping charge, the children of his love.

He's passed from earth, for evermore to be
Decked in the robes of immortality ;
Still for his flock full many a hallow'd deed
In odor-sweets from golden censers plead.

He's passed away—his soul-directing light
Has set within the tomb's unconscious night ;
He's passed to realms by saints and angels trod—
Passed from the footstool of the throne of God.

LINES.

TO ——

HOW sweet is Friendship's angel breath,
   Perfumed by flowers of living love ;
How fair its ever-during wreath,
   Plucked in Affection's scented grove ;
How deep the dream of priceless worth
   To which they e'er the soul incline—
That breath, that wreath, of all on earth, are
    yours,
   And O, that dream is mine !

LINES.

[Addressed to a traveling companion when separating from
him in Kentucky in the year 184–]

ABOVE the broad Ohio's limpid stream,
   On banks which kiss the morning's misty
      cloud
We sit, with tearful eye and anxious ear
To list the tolling bell and heaving sweep
Which speak the lab'ring steamer, as adown
To Southern markets, laden with the hopes
And various produce of these Western wilds
She onward moves.
   We sit, we list, we weep—to-day we part
To breast alone the ocean-waves of care.
Rocked in the storm-tost cradle of the past
We've dreamed together a fond morning dream,
While Hope still spread out its delusive chart
To point the hills of Fame, whose mystic front
Rose up in golden grandeur, and enlarged ·
By Fancy's wild and dreamy telescope,
Immortal seemed.
   But now our dreams are o'er, and Memory
Becomes the sepulchre, from which alone

The shadowy ghosts of our departed hopes
Will rise, commingled with the scenes and thoughts
And fairy palaces which Fancy built
Upon the airy heights and changing sands
Of that wild Isthmus which alone connects
"The Past and Future—two Eternities"—
And rolls the Present back upon the Past.

   We've met, and now we part—to meet again !
But whether on the treacherous shores of Time,
Or in the regions of a world unknown
We cannot tell : but yet, not Lethe's stream,
Nor time, nor care, nor dark disease, nor death
Shall blot remembrance from the cherished page
Of thoughts, the record of the things that were.

   Bright be thy scenes in future life—thy path
With rich perfumes of innocence and peace
Be rendered pleasant ! And may angels guard
Thee and the fair one plighted to be thine !

*   *   *   *   *   *   *

THE GREEK SLAVE.

[The following lines were written on looking at that celebrated piece of Statuary in which Powers has combined the
perfection of human shape with the emotions of a captive
maid exposed for sale in a Turkish Slave Market. " The
cross and locket seen in the folds of her drapery show her
to be a Christian and beloved."]

TORN from the charms of home, a slave she
    stands,
  And nude, to charm the Moslem's lustful eye ;
Fair as the fairest of the Houri bands
  That breathe delight in his Elysian sky.

Alone she stands, and with averted glance :
  Her gentle thoughts go back to other days,
And kindle in her soul a holy trance,
  Pure as the light from uncreated rays.

The Turk appears—he seeks a youthful fair,
  His passion's treasure and perfection's prize ;
But all subdued by virtue's peerless air,
  Worship, not passion, kindles in his eyes.

That youthful maiden's half disdainful glance—
    That meek imploring look, that modest charm,
That Christian calmness check the rude advance,
    And save the maiden from impending harm.

Beauty has triumphed there, for Virtue's soul
    Has cast its charm o'er that expressive face,
While Genius lent its spirit's high control,
    To mould the shield of a protective grace.

O, THINK NOT THAT I DO NOT FEEL!

[In the spring of 18—, a brother of the author's was drowned in Wallace River, Nova Scotia, leaving a beloved wife and one child, a little girl about eight years old. After the accident it was observed that the child did not cry, and her mother, half chidingly, asked her the reason. Her answer was, " I feel as much as any of you can feel, and yet —*I cannot cry !*"]

O THINK not that I do not feel
    Because I cannot cry !
There is a grief which may congeal
    The moisture of the eye ;
A grief so deep that it can chill
    The fountains of the soul,
And freeze the gushings of that rill
    Which laves life's golden bowl.

I feel that there was once a smile
    For me, which is no more,
And fairy visions nurst the while,
    Which visions now are o'er !·
I feel that there was once a hand
    To clasp me to a breast,
Now, cold and lifeless, in that land
    Where all the weary rest.

I feel that—oh ! too much I feel !—
    And tears would bring relief,
For every trickling sphere would steal
    A portion of my grief.
Though tearless, think not I the less
    Do feel the weight of gloom,
For Sorrow, with its rude caress,
    Hath made my heart its tomb !

NOTHING TO EAT.

NOTHING to eat ! 'tis the wailing cry
   That starvelings utter in deep despair,
When they stretch themselves in pain to die,
   All lost to hope ; too weak for prayer.
Nothing to eat ! the chainless mind
In famine becomes confused and blind ;
A thousand phantoms before it rise,
Mocking it still with taunting cries ;
Luring it off where the demons reign ;
Every change is a change of pain ;
Still in its madness it will repeat—
Nothing to eat ! Nothing to eat !

Who will tell us of "Nothing to Wear."—
   The gilded falsehood of Fashion's queen—
Of " Nothing to do "—" to say "—" to spare "—
   They're all as naught to the cry, I ween,
Which starving ones in their pain repeat—
Nothing to eat ! Nothing to eat !

In a lonely garret a mother lies :
Draw near, and look at those fearful eyes—
They were Beauty's once ! Those lips so pale
And those sunken cheeks tell a mournful tale

Of the change which hunger and care can bring
When they prey on the fair with united sting.
That starving mother and starving child !—
They are dying now—how strange and wild
Are their every look ! Bring bread and wine !
Come, lonely mother, arouse and dine !—
Ah ! they're brought too late from the board of
  wealth
To bring back that mother to hope and health !
Though she seems to feast with her fearful eyes ;
   As if she fain would again be strong ;
That bread and wine are a tempting prize
   To one with nothing to eat so long.

Alone a maiden is on the street,
   A poor, a friendless, a homeless one :
The freezing wind and blinding sleet
   Career like anger at set of sun.
Where shall she go ?   Ah ! who can tell ?
Hunger and pride in her thoughts rebel.
How hard it is to restrain her pride—
How hard to ask and to be denied !
Thousands around her have wealth untold,
Treasures of silver and treasures of gold,
While thousands like her have nothing to eat,
Starving in garrets or on the street.
The rich pass on without thought or care,
And if alms are asked they've nothing to spare :
They can spare to folly, can spare to pride,
Can spare to fashion, but woe betide

The hungry beings who dare entreat,
Because, forsooth, they've nothing to eat.
So the rich pass on to some gilded show,
They've nothing to spare to the poor and low.

Alone a maiden is on the street,
   A poor, a friendless, a homeless one ;
In the freezing wind and the blinding sleet,
   She asks herself what *shall* be done ?
With beauty and virtue her only store ;
   She ponders of them as she treads alone
From street to street, and from door to door :
   She has " asked for bread and received a stone."
What shall be done ?   What shall be done ?
Ah ! poor and lonely and friendless one !
Shall we judge thee harshly when hunger pleads,
   And hope has proved a deceitful tale,
If thy answer be given in evil deeds,
   When evil deeds can alone avail ?

Come, stately queen of the marble hall,
Pride of a " circle," belle of the ball ;
A stranger to even a single care,
With costly raiment and jewels rare,
And more than enough to eat and wear,
Thou must have a tender heart indeed ;
   An open hand when the hungry call ;
A willing ear when the helpless plead,
   And love for thy fellow creatures all.
Yet why didst thou spurn from thy marble hall

The starving maiden that asked for bread?
That act of thine was a deed of thrall ;
   It ended hope and to ruin led !
To whom should a maid in distress appeal,
If a sister's heart prove hard as steel—
If a sister's voice can bid her go,
All reckless of ruin or woman's woe,
And call her unjustly in words of shame,
A thing of evil too vile to name ?

Ah ! when thus branded'and coldly spurned,
Is it strange that the maiden in madness turned,
As a last resource to the vile and rude,
And bartered her virtue—her all—for food ?

Come, stately queen of the marble hall,
   If angels are glad when the vile reform,
Should'st thou take part in a sister's fall
   By driving her forth in a night of storm ?
Remember that thousands as fair, as proud,
And as pure as thou, have weakly bowed,
Like erring frailties, at Passion's shrine—
Have tasted its manna and drunk its wine,
With no excuse but a wanton will
   To lead them in error's corrupting way ;
They yield, but, in yielding, make efforts still
   To hide their deeds from the light of day.

Nothing to eat ! 'tis the fearful cry
   Of wild, united, half frantic men
Who throng the streets. The sound swells high—
   Nothing to eat !—again !—again !

What means it ?   These are the men of toil—
Why do they riot and cry for spoil ?
Why do they batter the storehouse down,
And scatter abroad through the hungry town
The unbought food which in frantic might
They wrest by force, without thought of right ?
It is—that Toil is no more repaid
By perishing food in the marts of trade ;
That men are starving ; that children moan ;
That hunger is stronger than walls of stone.
They are starving fathers who throng the street ;
Their wives and children have nothing to eat !

Nothing to eat ! 'tis the burning thought
    Of shipwrecked men on the ocean wave ;
Their foundered vessel the depths has sought,
    And still around them the waters rave.
A crazy raft is their sole support ;
    Hunger increases as hope decays ;
The gull sweeps round them as if in sport,
    And nearer and nearer the dolphin plays.
    Thus has it been for days and days :
Their cheeks are sunken, their eyes are wild,
    Relief is distant, and famine preys
With increasing pang.   Ah ! one has smiled—
For him the sorrows of life are past ;
The wail of the sea, the sigh of the blast,
No more are heard.   His nerves no more
Shrink back in torture.   A fairer shore

Than earth can boast, like a dream, is spread
In the airy realms where the seraphs tread.
Oh ! it were bliss on such shores to stray,
And angels whisper—" Away ! away !"

Another mutters of nothing to eat,
   And stares at his fellows with wolfish eyes :
His thoughts are fiends, which would fain entreat
   For human flesh when a comrade dies.
He curses himself—his God.   He raves
At the warring winds and the warring waves ;
He curses his fellows, as if they viewed
In him a beast, to be slain for food ;
Then leaps in the flood, like a demon grim,
And swears none ever shall feast on him.

More calmly others await their doom,
   Though every day makes their number less :
A moment seems like an age of gloom,
   With such surroundings, in such distress.
At length a hurricane sweeps the main :
   They sink ; but still in their thoughts repeat
The echoes lone of that sad refrain—
   " Nothing to eat !   Nothing to eat !"

NEW ORLEANS, *October*, 1857.

THE WAYS OF CHRISTENDOM.

A translation from the Japanese of Kram Yengib.

[Our readers will remember that a few natives of Japan were brought to this country by the Japan expedition sent out some years since by the United States Government. One of them, Kram Yengib, has since returned to his native land and published a satirical poem on the Church, the Government, and the social condition of Christendom. The following is a translation:]

INTRODUCTION.

FORGIVE me, O, my lovely native isle,
  Fair Crescent gem set in the em'rald sea,*
For I have wandered out beyond thy smile,
  And would return, a suppliant, to thee :
Forgive me, if thou can'st, and I shall be
  No more an exile in barbaric lands,

* Nipon, the principal island of Japan, the birthplace of Yengib, is semi-lunar in shape, and as the sea around it is shallow, its color of course is green. The sea is blue only where its depth is very great.

Where warring Christians ever disagree,
    And Might the majesty of Right withstands,
And Wealth exemption claims from Law's most
        stern commands.

My crime was great—a wish to wander forth—
    "My punishment is more than I can bear :"
From the far West unto the frozen North
    I've passed—a dreary pilgrimage—to share
With Christian dogs in their unholy fare
    Of bullock's flesh, and other vile compounds ;
To witness villanies 'twere sin to spare,
    And listen to those senseless, soulless sounds
That Christians worship call—a worship which
        confounds.

But I will sing of all that I have seen,
    So that no more a heav'n blessed Japanese
May wish to wander forth where I have been,
    And tempt the fury of accursed seas
    With sinful hopes of happiness and ease—
Hopes, baseless, as they stretch beyond the isles
    Protected by our prophet's high decrees—
Who can expect Religion's holy smiles
When wandering over lands which Christian faith
        defiles ?

I.

THE CHURCH.

First, of the Church. Great Buddha! now inspire
My pen of steel with true poetic fire,
So that it may with faithful skill reveal
The monster curse, which on the public weal
Weighs like an incubus—assuming still
A thousand shapes to work its ends of ill.
The Church! Religion! these are magic words,
In Christian mouths, and forth they fly, as birds,
Blue-winged and bound to heaven—but in their
  train
Are raven-croakings and the lust of gain !

All from one Book their various teachings draw,
And all acknowledge the same moral law ;
Yet, in their creeds they strangely disagree,
And as they bend in prayer the pliant knee,
A curse is hurled at each opposing creed,
And Vengeance vows that heretics should bleed.

Of leading tenets, held as orthodox,
Some we may mention as the sacred rocks
On which the creeds of Christendom are based :
These are—one God, or three in one embraced ;
One Devil, with a countless demon-train ;
Immortal life—which may prove loss or gain ;

The eating of an apple from a tree,
And its result—complete depravity;
One Heaven, the refuge of a chosen few;
One Hell, the birthright of that damned crew,
The many, who must writhe for endless ages
In burning sulphur lakes, predestined wages
For being "born in sin" without their knowledge,
And for neglecting to attend the college
Where Grace imparts its lessons of repentance,
Which can alone avert the "dreadful sentence."

On these foundation stones strange structures
    rise,
Whose spires are pointing proudly to the skies;
Each one proclaims itself the only "true,"
And vainly boasts—"I'm holier than you!"
While all alike are bound by Error's chains,
Whose rust corrosive Truth's fair vestment stains.

That the meek Founder of the Christian plan
Gave moral teachings as the guide of man,
Can never be denied.   He taught that Love
Was the great lever to raise men above
The grovelings of earth; that wealth should be
Despised as filthy dross; that man should flee
Temptation's luring paths; that human pride
To sorrow and destruction was allied;
That hatred was accursed, and that "to do
To others as you'd have them do to you,"
Was the great law of life.

Such simple rules—
Too high for men ; too holy for the schools—
(Unlike our Buddha's easier commands,)
Have spread hypocrisy o'er Christian lands ;
And now that " leaven of the Pharisees "
Remains, the putrid and corrupting lees
Of the "new wine " which promised peace and
    heaven,
And which, that all might drink and live, was
    given.
Thus Christian rights became an empty show,
And Christian deeds the deeds of foe to foe ;
Sect hating sect, prays for each others fall,
Till rivalry and envy rule in all.

Priests are employed to have the care of souls,
Just as the sexton is employed, who tolls
The sinner-calling bell.   They preach for gold ;
Their services, like merchant's wares, are sold.
On sumptuous fare they live, and solemn pride
They wrap around them, as a cloak, to hide
Their grosser failings.   Are these, then, the guides
Whom a just heaven, or yellow dust provides ?
Are these the teachers who take up the cross—
Who look on wealth as worse than filthy dross—
Who, without purse or scrip, or ordered plan,
Go forth to " preach glad tidings " unto man ?
Are these the kind, the humble and the pure,
Who would contempt and buffetings endure,

All for their Master's sake ?   Are these the meek
Who, if opposed and smitten on one cheek,
Would turn the other also ?   Seek the fane
Whose gilded turrets point to heaven in vain ;
Mark its rich trappings and its cushioned pews
Where wealthy Christians meet at times to muse
On business and exchange—the ways of trade—
How bubbles float—how millionaires are made—
How queenly beauties make so grand a show—
How in some eyes such witching glances glow—
How love is nursed—while not a thought is given
To laying up fair treasure stores in Heaven,
Where thieves can ne'er approach.   Let priests
      attend
To all such ghostly business, and befriend
Their paying patrons !   They the brokers are
Betwixt the seen and unseen—near and far—
And for cash paid in hand, a goodly sum,
They sell exchange upon " the world to come !"

    Thus do the priests of faith " make merchan-
      dise,"
Till worldly wealth and power become their prize ;
Each creed has its anointed devotees,
Who feast on fatness, and in honored ease
Make proud, presumptuous prayers.   To Him on
      high
They talk as to some equal in the sky ;
They tell Him what to bless and what to spurn—
" We bless thee, Lord, now bless us in return !"

This is their orison: Some dare pretend
That the decrees of highest Heaven will bend
At their request ; that they can loose or bind,
In earth or Heaven, as they may feel inclined—
Absolve from sin, and give to lust free reign
By kind "indulgence," when it yields them gain.
Others grow rich on tithes—Lord Bishops they—
Their word is law, and laymen must obey.
With princely "livings"—power in Church and
          State—
E'en among great ones they are doubly great.
Thousands must toil, must starve, perchance, to
          swell
Their golden treasures ; and if one rebel,
The willing bailiff and the jailer stern
Force him with due submission to return,
And ask admittance to the sacred fold
With that sure passport—penitential gold !
Others again, make faith a blind belief
In effete forms and visages of grief ;
While others still on holy works depend,
As if they could by "filthy rags "* ascend
The highest heav'n, and claim an honor'd seat
Where but "the pure in heart" their God can
          meet.

Thus all have forged their fetters for the mind,
And proved themselves blind leaders of the blind ;

* "And all our righteousness is as filthy rags."—*Scripture.*

Creed fights with creed, as crime contends with
    crime,
And each the other sullies o'er with grime.
Church speaks to church, but each conflicting call
Awakes the echoes of some prison wall ;
Nor is it strange—that wild, commingled cry—
For crimes and creeds together multiply.
These contradictions among Christian creeds
Have fostered unbelief and evil deeds.
Faith ne'er can be content with empty forms,
Hope's pinions fail 'mid theologic storms,
And soaring souls, to Deity allied,
Can ne'er, like swine, with husks be satisfied.

    And so poor Christians—Christians but in name,
Have lost in sects their singleness of aim :
Some seek amid the wiles of unbelief,
For present comfort—infidel to grief,
And pain, and joy, and all beyond the grave—
They bid defiance to the Stygian wave.
Others espouse new-fangled heresies,
Invent new prophecies, and new decrees,
And, like a prairie-fire, their doctrines spread,
For fools will follow where deceivers tread.
Thus Mormonism took its lustful rise,
And newer isms, fresh showered from the skies
By disembodied sprites, who come to rave
Of those strange lands which lie beyond the grave.
The Mormons have their prophets and their wives;
They sow licentiousness, a plant which thrives

In the rank soil which human hearts afford,
And yields a fruit by rascal "saints" adored.
But spirit-isms take a far wider range,
Pass through supernal lands in search of change ;
Seek out fair beauties of celestial mould,
Where spirit-spheres their spirit-fruits unfold—
Thrill with celestial love ; and still, aspire
To something fairer, purer, grander, higher !
Yet while these isms so wonderfully climb,
Like spirit-felons, into spheres sublime,
Their grand interpreters in earthly schools
Are dancing tables, animated stools,
And cupboards which can syllable by raps
The history of marvelous mishaps,
And tell the wonders of the heavenly host
Through the obsession of some gossip-ghost.

Compared with these, how pure the Buddhist
creed
So kindly suited to the sinner's need :
All who prove false should straight be sent to
dwell
Amid the tortures of the Christian's hell.

II.

GOVERNMENT.

In Christian lands all government is fraud—
The toiling millions have to kiss the rod ;
And while they clap their hands and shout,
    "we're free !"
Their limbs are galled by chains and slavery.
To him that hath is given.   The great take all—
While the poor wretch must starve, or humbly
    crawl,
After his strength is wasted, to the grave,
With none to pity him and none to save.
Grand are the titles by which rulers reign—
Dark are the deeds by which their souls they stain.
Kings, Emperors forsooth ! bend low the knee,
And homage yield to titled lechery !
Might robes itself in purple, and the sword
Leaps from its scabbard if a royal word
Of vengefulness is uttered.   Minions come !
Let the loud trump be sounded ; beat the drum ;
While the great cannon thunders to the sky :
Europe, thy balance bends beneath a fly !
    Thus Christian wars arise, and " peace on earth "
Is mocked at and profaned by " men of birth."
Let the base millions bleed and bleeding fight—
For " right divine " has wrongs which it must
    right,

And rights which are but human must give way
That rights divine can have unquestioned sway'!
    O, it doth pain me to the soul, to see
The vassalage of men who should be free.
" Outside barbarians" though they are, their wrongs
Speak to my judgment, as with cloven tongues
From which the blood is dropping. Let me grieve,
For I must pity though I can't relieve.
    " Ours is a land of laws" these Christians cry,
And that it is, the bard will not deny.
But oh, such laws ! Confused, conflicting, vain,
As the wild flights of a distempered brain,
Where "rotten burroughs" taint the moral air
And party-bribes for party-spoils prepare.
The mushroom legislator grossly thrives,
And claims control of property and lives.
By fraud elected, what but fraud should be
The groundwork of his partial polity ?
He meets his fellows—"honorable men,"
For such they humbly style themselves—and then
In Parliament assembled, laws they frame
To tax the toiler and th' unruly tame.
A fiction of these laws makes all men stand
Before them equal—brothers hand in hand—
But stern experience gives damning proof
That partial justice flies the poor man's roof
To wanton in a palace. Laws which change
With each revolving year must e'er be strange

Unto the toiling millions who must bow
As does the ox, when harnessed to the plow.
Hence lawyers must be feed to make that plain,
Which should be plain without them.   Sweat of
    brain
They give for gold, and guilt or purity
Is all the same to them :   Who pays goes free.
    This, of a land whose fame is fairest held
Among these Christian spoilers.   Now impelled
By curious quest we'll cross the sounding sea
To that great Western "land of liberty"—
That land of prairies wide and flowing streams,
Whose virgin soil with varied produce teems.
Columbia, hail !   On thee, heaven faintly smiles,
As if a gleam from our celestial isles
Had wandered off, and sought thy distant shore,
There to abide and brighten evermore.
But e'en Columbia, as a Christian land,
Is curst by Christian guile.   Would that the
    hand
Of Buddha might on its fair fields be laid,
So they might rest beneath his sacred shade !¦
In theory its government is pure ;
In practice 'tis corrupt.   There is no cure
For the gross ulcers which mine all within,
Filling the land with avarice and sin.
Free, universal suffrage is proclaimed,
That guilt may triumph and the truth be shamed.
The pot-house plotters meet in caucus vile
To lay their plans of selfishness and guile.

" Intrigue and bargain !" these the lusty twain
By which they triumph and by which they stain
The sacred robe of justice, which should be
Pure as the pearls which slumber 'neath the sea.
Elections are a fraud.   The public voice
Is cheated and deluded in its choice,
And where the best and wisest should be first,
Election takes the wickedest and worst.
The bribe-bought ballot gives the right to rule,
Though cast by grossest knave or dullest fool—
And fools and knaves, it must be understood,
Outnumber, ten to one, the wise and good.
        Thus Christian statesmen their republics frame ;
They manage them as gamblers do their game,
Making the knave a trump, and by their deal
Contrive, in seeming honesty, to steal.
The Press with them becomes a servile thing,
That puffs for pay, and makes its plaudits ring
For party candidates.   What's black or white,
To those who under party trammels write ?
The Bar's alike depraved.   O, draw not nigh
To where blind justice holds her balance high,
For though your cause may be as pure as heav'n,
You may be sure 'twill be against you giv'n.
False witnesses are purchasable things ;
And the paid pleader who against you brings
His score of such is sure of his reward ;
Against his shafts no honesty can guard.
Then the packed juror, with his bribe in hand :
None can his guilty agency withstand,

For ready to obey the legal beck,
He coolly holds eleven peers in check,
Making a farce of all the forms of law
That guilt, its coveted rewards, may draw.
  Oh, blessed Buddha ! that thou may'st forgive
The wand'ring bard, who scarce deserves to live,
I of those fierce barbarian-Christians write,
That ne'er again from liberty and light
A Japanese may stray !   Let full content
O'er our celestial realm be kindly sent,
And where barbaric splendors would allure,
Let Christian guilt become a speedy cure.

III.

SOCIAL CONDITION OF CHRISTENDOM.

In Christian lands falsehood's the only truth,
Deceit sits throned e'en on the brow of youth,
Masking pretention with its smooth disguise,
And making love with simulated sighs.
Fashion and folly rule the giddy throng
With gilded shows ; and e'en the poet's song,
Which should be high as heaven, finds its low rhyme
In vulgar teachings and ignoble crime.
Woman's a plaything, passionate, depraved,
By need, and greed, and vanity enslaved ;

While man, the Christian, filled with demon guile,
Still plays the fiend and murders with a smile.
Forgive me, Buddah,—great, eterne, supreme !
I sing of things, strange as a troubled dream ;
Of human beings in a form divine,
Who crawl like serpents through corruption's slime,
And then their boasted purity proclaim,
Deaf to rebuke ; insensible to shame !
From regal halls where courtly Fashion reigns,
To the low dens where fear alone restrains,
There are degrees in form but not in deed ;
The same dark fruit springs from the same vile seed.
In circles which are called "select" and "high,"
Honor's a bawd and courtesy a lie,
And rules akin in grosser forms prevail
Through lower levels of the social scale.
Call Friendship on the stage. Its warmest glow
Chills 'neath misfortune into Alpine snow.
To purple and fine linen it may bow ;
Castles of Indolence it may endow,
But from "chill penury" it stands aloof,
And still denies the shelter of its roof.
The flash of diamonds and the gleam of gold
May rouse its envy, but they still will mould
Its outward show—the letter of its grace—
Though of its spirit they retain no trace.
Call up the man of trade. Deceptive wares,
Adulterated drinks, and hidden snares
In every form of fabric, test the skill
Of Christian genius in its love of ill.

The wooden nutmeg and the oaken ham*
Are only grosser forms of that great sham,
Which palms off tinsel for true cloth of gold,
And makes the coward master of the bold.
Commerce its bubbles hath, its flying kites,
Its men of straw, that swagger forth as knights
And merchant princes—mockeries sublime
Which touch the hollow tympanum of time.

In social converse the same rule obtains ;
Deception hides, as best it can, the stains
Which mark the inner life. From " not at home,"
A petty falsehood, light as airy foam—
To the vile depths, where honor shrinks, aghast,
And all the barriers of truth are passed,
The way is strewn by arts of false pretense
Which bid all honesty and virtue hence !

Let Love come in the list.   Can it redeem
The darker features of the poet's theme ?
Can its great truths o'ershadow the deceit
Which turns to bitterness what should be sweet ?
Not in these Christian lands, where hearts are sold,
Where an " establishment " and hoarded gold
Outweigh affection.   Not where solemn vows
Are held as light as air, and but arouse
A wanton spirit ; making young desire
The very nurse of an unhallowed fire.

---

* It is confidently stated that in one of the Christian
States deception is carried to such an extent that spurious
hams, nutmegs, and other articles of a like character, are
manufactured of wood.

The Christian's love is passion's unchecked course,
Or that base barter, where affection's force
Is lost in selfish aims.   There is no truth
Where love is not ; no fond prophetic youth ;
But in their stead cold calculations rise
And truest wisdom seems the most unwise.
  . Buddah, supreme !   I bow before thy throne.
A wanderer returned, I humbly own
The folly of my course.   To thy strong arm
My weakness owes its strength. Still free from harm
I mingled with barbarians, fierce and wild,
And touched their pitch, but still, was not defiled.
In adoration meek, I bow the knee,
And cry Japan, Buddha, and Liberty !

MY BROTHERS' GRAVES.

[Written at the request of a lady whose two brothers died
of injuries received on the battle-fields of Mexico.]

MY brothers' graves !—my brothers' graves !
　　Dear spots where lov'd ones rest ;
Where sunshine smiles and verdure waves,
　　And where the song-bird's nest
Is built among the flowers which cheer
The lengthened summer of the year.

Though from each other distant far,
　　And distant far from me,
I oft times speed in fancy's car
　　These hallowed spots to see—
To feel " the joy of grief," and weep
O'er the green hillocks where they sleep.

Too early lost !　In glory's race
　　They sought the battle plain,
And early found, in death's embrace,
　　A balm for every pain :
One fell beneath Jalapa's sky,
The other sought his home—to die.

And both are gone—the kind, the good,
  The loving and the brave,
And still at noon the waving wood
  Casts shadows o'er each grave,—
And the blue sky looks calmly on,
Nor seems to weep that they are gone.

And why should I ?—a world of care,
  Perchance, a world of woe,
If living, they would have to share,
  Which, dead, they cannot know.
These truant tears of mine I'll dry—
My brothers live with Him on high.

SOLITUDE.

ALL gently breathes the voice of Solitude !
      It gives its whispers to the spirit's ear
In eloquence so tender and subdued,
      That the rapt seraphs might descend to hear.
And with the teachings of that gentle voice
      There comes a deep forgetfulness of care,
Till the freed soul with Nature can rejoice,
      And pluck fresh garlands, ever pure and fair.

No grosser sound of earth can e'er be heard
      Where Solitude asserts her gentler sway,
But, fairer than the wings of Eden's bird,
      Fancy her own unfolds and floats away,—
Away, away, to those fair lands of bliss,
      Rich with the flow'rets of expanded thought—
The Edens of the soul—where from the kiss
      Of heaven-born muses Poesy is caught.

These are the treasures Solitude imparts !
      Oh, blissful visions of the flow'ry land,
Where the warm life-blood of poetic hearts
      All vital flows at Song's supreme command.

Come ! Be my chosen prize ! On willing wing
I'll flee the crowded haunts of grief and care,
To seek the climes where Thought's ideal spring,
Bequeaths its fragrance to Love's balmy air.

LINES TO ——

L ADY, for thee I seize my untried lyre,
　　And, with love's daring, touch its trembling
　　　　strings,
For thou my young ambition dost inspire,
　　And giv'st to fancy hope's upsoaring wings.
Cheer with thy smile, and all the world may lower,
　　For in thy smile a sunshine to my soul
Comes, with a blissful and ideal power,
　　And through bright vistas points a star-lit goal.
Joyous and blest be all thy future life,
　　Crowned with spring flow'rs and autumn's
　　　　golden fruit :
Far, far from thee be blighting care and strife,
　　And near, *one loving heart—one faithful lute !*

ON THE DEATH OF AN

AGED CLERGYMAN.

HIS voice is hushed ! In a last lone sleep
    His eyelids are closed forever,
And, shepherdless now, his flock may weep,
      But in hope. That sleep,
      So fearfully deep,
Cannot long the righteous sever !

When the trumpet sounds, and the dead arise,
    His spirit shall then, ascending,
Meet the sainted hosts of the upper skies—
      The blest—that rise
      " Where the treasure lies,"
In the land of love unending.

His priestly garb he shall wear no more,
    Though he kept it bright and stainless ;
But a richer garb, on a fairer shore,
      Shall forevermore
      Shed its lustre o'er
His spirit, released and chainless.

For half of a century his years
   He has spent as a people's pastor ;
He has borne the burdens and wiped the tears
     Of the young in years,
     Of the old, whose fears
  Made them tremble amid disaster.

For half of a century his life,
   As a sacred trust, was given
To a church on earth ; still he calmed the strife
     With which earth-born life
     Is forever rife,
  Till he passed to the church in heaven.

LINES TO ——.

[Written at one o'clock, A. M., on the morning of the
first of January, 1849.]

LADY, one song for thee ! I touch my lyre,
    As if the dear ambition of my soul
Could find in it an echo.   Let me weave
Together wreaths of sweetest harmony,
Still thou shalt be the music of my verse,
And lend thy spirit to my fairest dreams !
        E'en now, when thought takes wing,
To soar in fancy o'er the fields of hope,
Thou'rt the companion of my wayward flight,
Else, all my course were dark.   But when thou art
Twin wanderer through fancy's fairy realm,
The cheering iris spans hope's highest heaven,
And paints its promises with richest dyes.
O, 'tis delightful !—haply, but a dream,
Yet would I not forego such blissful dreams
For all of loveless wealth's realities.
Here, on the altar of the infant year
I cast the votive off'ring !   May the glow
Of fond affection give the incense flame,
And warm the censer with love's blest delight.

LINES.

[Written at sea in a friend's Scrap-book.]

O'ER passion's wave let reason guide
   The bark which bears us on ;
God guard the rudder—still the tide,
And land us safely, side by side,
So we may evermore abide
   Near his Eternal Throne !

LITTLE WILLIE.

I WILL sing no song of sorrow,
  Though my flow'r has ceased to bloom,
And the solemn winds of autumn
  Sigh their dirge above his tomb—
For my Willie! O, my Willie!
  Was a child of love and light,
And the world to which he's journeyed
  Never can be one of night.

Willie was our young immortal,
  Blessing earth a little while,
With the freshness of his spirit,
  And the glory of his smile ;
But the golden gates of heaven
  Opened wide to let him in,
And a seraph's hymn of welcome
  Called him from this world of sin.

So our Willie has departed
  Bearing not a stain of earth,
And though painful was the parting,
  'Twas to him " a second birth."

Sinless, to the realms eternal
   He has borne a mother's prayer,
And in dreams of bliss supernal
   I have met his spirit there.

NEW ORLEANS, *Oct.* 15, 1865.

O, LET ME DREAM.

O LET me dream those dreams again—
    The dreams of long ago—
When all my hopes had angel wings,
And, in my path, the crystal springs
    Of life were in their flow.
O, let me dream those dreams again—
    The dreams of long ago !

O, let me dream those boyhood dreams,
    Which bathed my soul in light,
When, playing in life's sunny bowers,
I twined a chaplet wreath of flowers
    For one so fair and bright—
For one who is an angel now—
    An angel robed in white.

O, let me dream those dreams again !
    The past bring back once more :
I ask it on my bended knees—
O let those mystic memories
    Unlock their golden store,
So I can touch them one by one
    And count my treasures o'er.

O, let me dream those dreams again,
   Which came ere grief and care
Had placed their signet on my brow—
And bound me to a sterner Now
   That goads and will not spare,—
I'd dream of her who, although dead,
   Is still so pure and fair.

FOR THEE, MY LOVE, FOR THEE !

A LYRIC.

THY love's the sun, thou peerless one—
  It warms me with its glow ;
With light divine it seems to shine,
  Though I alone can know
Its secret charm—a shield from harm
  On life's uncertain sea:
O, I shall pray, both night and day,
  For thee, my love, for thee !

With starry gleams, in holy dreams
  Thou comest to my soul,
As o'er a strand of golden sand
  Life's sparkling waters roll :
And, with the kiss of purest bliss,
  Attuned to harmony,
My thoughts arise to brightest skies,
  With thee, my love, with thee.

The golden chimes of sweetest rhymes
   Thy charms but faintly tell,
The softest note that e'er did float
   From fairy horn or shell—
With birds that sing, and flow'rs of spring,
   And all bright things that be—
None can compare, with voice or air,
   With thee, my love, with thee !

O, I would write thy name with light,
   To shame the stars above,
And in high lays would ever praise
   The riches of thy love,
All wealth that shines in golden mines,
   All gems of land and sea,
Are but as rust and trampled dust,
   To thee, my love, to thee !

THE LIGHT OF MY LOVED ONE'S EYES.

Who will praise bestow
On the opal's glow,
Or the diamond's sparkling sheen,
When the richer prize
Of my loved one's eyes
May, in peerless pride, be seen ?
In each liquid sphere
Does a glow appear
That would light up the farthest skies,
For 'tis never night
When appears the light,
The light of my loved one's eyes—
The light of my loved one's eyes—
For 'tis never night
When appears the light,
The light of my loved one's eyes.

All the world seems gay
As the flow'rs of May,
When illumed by my loved one's smile,
For the blessed gleam,
Like a holy beam
From some blissful, starry isle,

With a lustre rare
Maketh all things fair
As the fairest of earth or skies,—
For 'tis never night
When appears the light,
The light of my loved one's eyes—
The light of my loved one's eyes—
For 'tis never night
When appears the light,
The light of my loved one's ones.

FORGETTING THEE?

FORGETTING thee ? oh no, my love :
   I never can forget
The pulse of joy that thrilled my heart
   When first we fondly met ;
The hope that kindled in the blaze
   Of thy soul-piercing eye,
And taught me how to worship thee—
   My all beneath the sky !
Nay, chide no more : I will confess,
   And thou my saint shall be,
And kneeling at thy feet I'll swear—
   I am for *getting* thee !

Forgetting thee ? When Spring forgets
   To robe the fields in bloom,
And, sere and desolate, my heart
   Shall all its hopes entomb ;
When light and joy shall to my soul
   Come as a deadly blight,
And stars no more shall brightly gem
   The azure halls of night,
I may forget, but not till then ;
   Still, thou my saint shall be,
And I'll confess—I am, my love,
   I am for *getting* thee !

OUT, OUT INTO THE SUNLIGHT.

OUT, out into the sunlight from the tyrant's
        dungeon wall;
Let man before his fellow man no longer fawn
        and crawl !
Accurs'd be hoary tyrannies, and more accurs'd
        be he
Whose traitor-hand would basely forge a fetter
        for the free !
        Out, out into the sunlight !

Out, out into the sunlight, from the darkened
        chamber where
The sick, with plaints of agony and feebly-uttered
        prayer,
Ask God to alter His decrees, and by his sov-
        'reign will
To utter a divine *"Be healed !"* or else a *"Peace,
        be still !"*
        Out, out into the sunlight.

Out, out into the sunlight, from the bigot's dark-
        some cell,
Where superstition plumes herself with mysteries
        from hell ;

Where mind is manacled with dread, and base
    unholy fears
Cast out all love and, in its stead, dig deep the
    fount of tears.
        Out, out into the sunlight !

Out, out into the sunlight, from the blackness of
    despair,
Where hope is lost, and weary souls, bow'd down
    by grief and care,
Find earth a barren desert-waste, and heav'n a
    starless wild,
And they themselves, poor creeping worms, un-
    cared for and defiled.
        Out, out into the sunlight !

Out, out into the sunlight, from the vampire hordes
    that draw
The life-blood from all better life, all equity from
    law ;
Who fill this goodly world of ours with discontent
    and strife,
And consecrate to godless deeds the pistol and
    the knife.
        Out, out into the sunlight !

Out, out into the sunlight, from those rayless
    depths of gloom,
Which hide alike all peace on earth, and peace
    beyond the tomb ;

Where feeble toilers toil in tears to find their
    struggles vain,
And curse the Pow'r that made their lives a herit-
    age of pain.
        Out, out into the sunlight!

Out, out into the sunlight, where the soul, re-
    deemed and free,
Can borrow wings from heav'nly hopes : with
    eyes of faith can see
Beyond the shadows of the tomb the morning-
    land appear
Where peace, and love, and joy shall crown the
    never-ending year.
        Out, out into the sunlight!

THE GOLDEN CHAIN.

[Written for the Odd Fellows' Anniversary Celebration.]

THERE is a chain whose golden links
    Heaven's choicest gifts embrace ;
Life's crowning-heritage on earth,
    Its glory and its grace :
Pure as the rainbow's blended dyes,
    Free as the stars from stain,
Are Friendship, Love, and Truth—the links
    Which form that golden chain.

FRIENDSHIP ! in mystic brotherhood
    It binds man to his kind,
Supporting still the poor and frail,
    And guiding still the blind.
So brave to meet fraternal wants,
    So gentle in distress,
It shares, it watches, and it cheers,
    And prays that Heav'n may bless.

LOVE ! blissful dream of Eden sweets
    Which angels fain would breathe ;
It comes like spring, the tree of life
    With blossoms to enwreathe ;

It presses from joy's blushing grapes
    Their rich ambrosial wine,
And thrills the throbbing human heart
    With ecstacies divine.

TRUTH ! mirror of the god-like mind !
    Like the unruffled lake,
Reflecting all the glowing heavens,
    Whose glories o'er it break.
In its clear depths no hidden snare
    Can ever lie concealed,
For all things there are pure and bright
    As Jove's immortal shield.

Thus richly linked the golden chain
    A sacred charm extends,
Inviting still the good and true
    To join for noble ends :
Making the *words* of brotherhood
    Assume a magic power,
And every *sign* a benison,
    And each *Degree* a dower.

So stands the glorious Order with
    Its banners fair unfurled,
Proclaiming Friendship, Love and Truth,
    Redeemers of the world ;
Keeping the sacred *jewels* bright
    Around which brothers meet,
And symbolizing holy ties
    With *water, flowers,* and *wheat.*

SONG OF WELCOME.

[Written for the General Convention of the Young Men's
Christian Association.]

WELCOME, brothers ! from the woodlands,
　　From the cities by the sea,
From the heaven-kissing mountains
　　Here we meet in unity.
Let us join the angel chorus,
　　Let us shout—again—again !—
" Glory be to God, the Highest !
　　Peace on earth ! Good will to men !"

Welcome, brothers !　Bonds fraternal
　　Make our hearts responsive beat ;
Giving strength to aid the erring ;
　　Rendering communion sweet.
Join we then the angel chorus,
　　Shouting loud—again—again !—
" Glory be to God, the Highest !
　　Peace on earth ! Good will to men !"

Welcome, brothers !   Strong in council ;
   May we prove in virtue brave ;
Brave to aid the broken-hearted—
   Strong to comfort and to save—
Swelling still the angel chorus,
   Shouting still—again—again !
" Glory be to God, the Highest,
   Peace on earth ! Good will to men !"

DOMESTIC FELICITY.

[A Scene from Real Life, between a fond husband and a would-be fashionable wife, who has a tongue, and uses it in a manner peculiar to herself.]

WILLIE.

COME to me, Flora; the earth hath no treasure
So dear unto me as the light of thy smile ;
Come, and these arms shall enfold thee as fondly
As waves when encircling some beautiful isle.

Come to me, dearest, and tell of thy sorrowings ;
Who hath annoyed thee, my darling, my wife ?
If it be woman, I'll fight all her brotherhood ;
If it be man, he shall pay with his life.

FLORA.

Why, dearest Willie, we ladies have miseries—
Sorrows unthought of, undreamed of by man—
You " coarser vessels " are still inconsiderate,
Though you may love us *as much as you can !*

Sensitive, delicate, highly poetical :
   Keenly we suffer as warmly we feel ;
Worthy of worship we are and angelical ;
   Down on your knees to me, down Willie, kneel.

What ! you refuse ? And shall I then recount to
     you
   Part of the catalogue, fearfully long,
Which is my proof that in love or in sorrow, we
   Gentle ones suffer much more than the strong ?

Strength is robustuous, earthy, tyrannical,
   Man has his fierceness in love as in hate,
But the true woman's all beauty and sympathy ;
   Meek as a flower, she bows to her fate.

See how resigned I am, never complainingly
   Vexing my Willie with tales of my woe !—
Suffer !—no tongue can tell how I am suffering,
   Yet my worst sorrows no mortal shall know !

There's Mrs. Money Purse—I do not envy her,
   Yet if you knew but how hard 'tis to bear
The flash of her diamonds, the whirl of her carriage
     wheels,
   Sure you would pity me, pity and spare.

Think of it, Willie, she's old and she's ugly too ;
   I, your true wife, am a beauty and young ;
If I were rich I should show you the difference,
   Then should my praises be said and be sung.

Men will have fashions and ladies must follow them,
　Follow, no matter how much it may cost,
Still must they struggle to keep up appearances !
　Think in those struggles how many are lost !

I'm your true wife, and I know of your poverty,
　Just then imagine how bad I must feel
When brocades and rich laces are shown at the
　windows,
　And I can but look in, and—turn on my heel !

I cannot buy them, and oh, the temptations
　Which virtuous poverty e'er must endure,
When, as in my case, it treads among pitfalls
　And never is certain its footing is sure.

WILLIE.

So you're tired of poverty, are you, my Flora ?
　Though not quite as poor as you were when we
　wed.
You fear some rich lion may enter our jungle,
　And you'll, like a lamb, to the slaughter be led.

Fear not, be a woman, and wealth will not tempt
　you ;
　Those lambs are too willing that run to the snare:
That virtue is tainted which welcomes temptation,
　If true, it the strongest of tempters may dare.

FLORA.

There now, that's the way with you, always up-
    braiding me,
    Flinging out coarse inuendoes and jeers ;
No wonder my cheeks are deprived of their roses,
    My eyes melt away in an ocean of tears.

You're a brute, and not even an angel could bear
    with you ;
    Oh, were I but back to my mother once more,
I'd find some one then who would know how to
    prize me ;
    Some man with a heart that could love and
    adore !

Pshaw ! it's no use to say you're too poor to sup-
    port me,
    For there's Mr. Jones who is poorer than you,
But he always can purchase a shawl or a bonnet,
    As all husbands can who are loyal and true.

If he only had now a sweet wife—such as I am—
    And not a mere stick ; a mere bundle of bones;
He'd wear out his fingers to load her with jewels,
    And show to the world how he prized Mrs.
    Jones.

Not a word ! not a word ! I insist on it, Willie,
    For I plainly perceive by the curl of your lip
That you're itching to say something vulgar and
    silly,
    To which, if a man, I'd respond with a whip.

There again ! getting cross, it is sadly provoking;
 Come, ask my forgiveness and don't be absurd ;
No pouting and showing your temper, dear Willie,
 For you know your sweet Flora *must have the
 last word.*

GIVE ME THE HARP.

[Mary A., a daughter of Rev. J. Blanchard, President of
Wheaton College, died on the 6th inst. She was a remarkably pious girl; and, as her spirit approached the heavenly
land, she cried out, " *Give me the harp I hear !*" and then
she quietly fell asleep in Jesus.]

GIVE me the harp with the sounding strings,
    The harp whose tones I hear—
It seems upborne by an angel's wings,
And unto my bursting heart it brings
    The sounds of hope and cheer—
A melody all divine, that springs
    From a higher and purer sphere.

Give me the harp, and this trembling hand
    Released from the ills of earth,
Shall learn the lays of the better land,
Shall touch the strings with a high command,
    And the joy of a spirit-birth
Shall thrill my soul with a rapture grand,
    With a fond and holy mirth.

Give me the harp, and I'll bid farewell
 To the fleeting scenes of time ;
With the loved ones gone before I'd dwell,
My harp with theirs should the echoes swell
 Of a high immortal rhyme ;
Give me the harp, for I fain would tell
 Of release from this world of crime.

LINES.

[On the death of Harry Stroud Caldwell, son of James.H. and the late Josephine Caldwell, of this city (N. O.)]

I.

Sweet prattler, thou hast gone ;
Gone to thy mother's loving arms again,
Gone to that home above the homes of men.

II.

And should we grieve for thee ?
Grief is the badge of weakness and distress ;
The Hand that gave in blessing we should bless.

III.

We mourn not when the sun
Sinks in the West, for in the morn 'twill rise
As thou hast risen—a glory to the skies.

IV.

Thou wert not left in pain
To pass a weary pilgrimage on earth ;
Eternal joy came with thy " second birth."

V.

Then no presumptuous tear
Should tell of sorrow when our joy should be
Full, as God's blessings to the soul set free.

THE COMING OF THE SPRING.

TO ———

WHEN wintry winds through leafless boughs
    Discordant dirges wail,
Like some great sorrow taking voice
    To tell its mournful tale,—
Then Hope's prophetic wisdom breathes
    Of Time, the fleet of wing,
And of the joys which always crown
    The coming of the Spring.

Oh, lovely Spring ! when vine and spray
    Bloom like the prophet's rod ;
When violets and daisies rise
    From out the virgin sod ;
When bird and insect, leaf and flow'r,
    Life's joyous anthem sing,
Who—who that feels can fail to bless
    The coming of the Spring !

Spring is the time for soaring thought—
    Spring is the time for love—
When flow'rs breathe out their fragrant sighs
    And music charms the grove ;

And, oh, in bliss my spirit soars :
   To thee, my love, I'd bring
Fair chaplets, rich as those which crown
   The coming of the Spring.

BROTHERS, ARISE.

[Read before the Southern Literary Society, at its Tenth
Anniversary Celebration, February 18, 1859.]

SEE, on Time's dial the shadows receding,
    Moving abashed from the pathway of light.
List, the evaugel of progress is pleading !
    Rise in your manhood—contend for the Right !
        Brothers, arise !
        Strive for the prize !
Run for the goal that's eternally bright !

Long we've contended with toil unavailing ;
    Gathering wealth, which is dross ere it's won ;
Seeking for happiness ; seeking and failing ;
    Feeding on husks, like the prodigal son.
        Brothers, arise !
        Strive for the prize !
The labor of Life should be manfully done.

Freighted with poison, the air which surrounds us
    Comes fetid and foul from the haunts of the vile;
Step where we will, the contagion confounds us;
    Oh, let us seek that which will not defile !
        Brothers, arise !
        Strive for the prize !
Shake off the trammels of passion and guile.

Thousands, alas, are enamored of ruin ;
   Downward they rush, like a stream to the sea ;
Vanity, folly and crime their undoing—
   Scarce do they utter a prayer to be free !
          Brothers, arise !
          Strive for the prize !
Be truly brave, and the tempter will flee.

Rise like the lark when his song to the morning
   Thrills with fresh joy all the pulses of air ;
Rise like the sun, when the hills he's adorning
   With emeralds, flowers, and all that is fair !
          Brothers, arise !
          Strive for the prize !
Strive for a guerdon 'twere glory to share.

Oh, for a song that would thrill as the lightning,
   Which rifts the dun cloud like the glance of a god!
Still purifying, refreshing and bright'ning
   The air that we breathe when we wander abroad.
          Brothers, arise !
          Strive for the prize !
Look up to heaven, not down to the clod !

Seek not the trinkets and baubles of Fashion ;
   To bodily grossness enslave not the soul :
March up the age, with the promptings of Passion
   Held, like a steed, by the reins of control.
          Brothers, arise !
          Strive for the prize !
The standard of Reason and Manhood unroll.

See, on Time's dial the shadows receding,
    Moving abashed from the pathway of light.
List, the evangel of Progress is pleading !
    Rise in your manhood—contend for the Right !
        - Brothers, arise !
        Strive for the prize !
Run for the goal that's eternally bright.

GONE.

He has gone !
Gone to realms of light unending,
Where the hymns of earth, ascending
Are with angel-peans blending
    As they circle round the Throne !

All the cares which gather'd round him,
While Time's earthly fetters bound him,
Disappeared, when Death had crown'd him
    With a glory not his own.

Oh, then, weep not that before us
He has joined the deathless chorus :
Still his spirit hovers o'er us ;
    Weep not, then, that he has gone !

Gone to realms of light unending,
Where the hymns of earth ascending,
Are with angel-peans blending
    As they circle round the Throne !

I'VE KISSED HER IN A DREAM.*

SHE moves along the crowded streets,
    A vision fair and bright ;
Her lustrous eyes outshine the stars
    Which gem the halls of Night.
Her lips are Love's delighted throne :
    Her cheeks twin roses seem ;
And oh, the bliss—the more than bliss—
    I've kissed her in a dream !

Her voice is music, and her step
    Is light as Zephyr's tread ;
'Tis Paradise where'er she is ;
    'Tis rapture to be led
By her soft hand through phantom-lands,
    Where love is all the theme ;
And oh, the bliss—the more than bliss—
    I've kissed her in a dream !

* This song has been set to music.

Let others praise their work-day loves,
    And pledge them in their wine,
Thought-blossoms, cull'd in fairy groves,
    I'll wreathe in song for mine.
She's fair as heav'n, and dear and pure
    As sunlight's primal beam ;
And oh, the bliss—the more than bliss—
    I've kissed her in a dream !

THE PARTING.

UPON a lawn, at early dawn,
   They stood, with tearful eyes—
The fair and gentle Annie Ware,
   And valiant Willie Wise.

"Willie," said she, most tenderly,
   "Will, will you still be true,
And will you fight as valiant knight
   And lover bold should do?"

"I will," said Will, his horse meanwhile
   Impatient of delay,
Began to neigh with stately pride
   For fear he might say nay.

"And oh, beware!" fair Annie cried,
   Her words half choked with sighs:
He soon replied, "I will be ware
   If you will but be Wise!"

A kiss was his reward, and then
   He mounted on his steed,
And for her sake determined to
   Do valiant deeds indeed.

In pearls the dew hung on the grass
   When thus he sighed adieu !
"And must I part, alas! alas !
   With such a lass as you ?"

NEW ORLEANS, *December*, 1863.

SONG OF THE NEW YEAR.

Hark ! 'tis the midnight chime,
Which speaks the march of Time,
And calls up gushing memories of the departed
        year ;
Still, as the music swells
High from sonorous bells
Hope draws her horoscope and visions bright ap-
        pear.

Grandly the train comes on ;
Not spectres pale and wan
Are those prophetic thoughts which make the
        future bright,
But, of supernal mould,
Decked in their robes of gold,
Come they, the harbingers of liberty and light.

One with it Science brings,
Science, too deep for Kings,
Wider than worlds in the circuit of its sweep.
Near as our souls are near ;
Dear, as our hopes are dear ;
Pure as the stars which are mirrored in the deep.

One, with persuasive voice,
Bids the oppressed rejoice,
And shouts the song of Freedom in the tyrant's
very ear ;
Shouts, till from hill and wold
Come forth the true and bold—
Come forth to battle armed with gun and sword
and spear.

One seems in faith to rise,
Seeking with earnest eyes
For Wisdom's ways of pleasantness and gentle
paths of peace :
These, as a golden road,
Lead to the blest abode,
Where all the weary-laden rest and earthly sor-
rows cease.

List to the prophet train,
Ye who have felt the pain,
The sorrow and the falsehood and the vanities of
life ;
List, and in faith be strong,
Braving the false and wrong,
Come forth and prove yourselves heroic in the
strife.

Shake off all slavish fears,
Nurst amid cares and tears,
When darkness rested on the world, an incubus
of gloom.

Rise in thy human might !
Strike for the true and right !
Then thou may'st look in hope beyond the silence
of the tomb.

Far from earth's prison bars
Bright homes beyond the stars
Welcome the ransomed who have shaken off the
clay—
Homes where the blessed meet;
Oh ! for the loved retreat,
Bathed in the radiance of an eternal day !

SCIENCE AND ART.

TIME had commenced his flight.   The eternal
  hills,
To the deep-sounding music of the spheres,
Were marshaled into place.   Old Ocean's bounds
And limits were determined, and the floods
Filled all his caves with an unceasing song,
Which rose and fell, to suit the dance of worlds.

 'Twas spring—Earth's primal spring—birds
  were abroad ;
The air was vocal with their hymns ; and flowers
Laughed, on the first unfolding of their sweets,
To greet the gladsome day.

 Eden was happy then.. No shade of ill
Had ever rested on her virgin bowers,
And angel visitants from their high homes
Approved and wondered at the gen'ral joy.

 Beside Euphrates' stream two youths reclined,
Half mortal, half immortal in their form.
Beauteous they were ; but unto human eyes

They wore a dim and unsubstantial shape,
Like the faint shadows of a passing dream.
Angels could see them ; and to such they seemed
A strange and undeveloped mystery—
The pride and glory of the coming time—
The wonder of the ages yet to be !
One, SCIENCE called, had a clear God-like brow,
And eyes, far-seeing, yet of gentlest cast ;
The other, ART, seemed the embodiment
Of every germ of skill and plastic power.
Alike, and still unlike ! As brothers, they
Spoke of their earthly mission. They surveyed
The work to each allotted, and agreed
That through the thought and by the hands of
    man
That work should be performed. Invisible,
They were to act a gentle prompter's part,
And by a spirit-chain of faith and love,
All humanized with emulative pride,
They were to lead men on to noble deeds
At which their peers should wonder and rejoice.

   Time passed. Earth's plains were peopled. Art
    commenced
The prefatory wonders of his work.
But at the first men's hands were slow to shape
The prompt designings of suggestive thought
Which came, they knew not whence. Soon Prac-
    tice gave
Fresh pliancy to every finger's joint,

Till, from the deep, dark caverns of the earth,
Ores were brought forth and moulded, as they list,
Who, tutored into cunning workmanship,
Could ply the hammer and could forge the steel.
Then the rude loom and the still ruder plough,
And arms for warfare, and the woodman's axe—
First fruits of labor and constructive skill—
Appeared and claimed a lasting meed of praise.
Science looked on, well pleased.   In the deep earth
From which the ores were taken, caverns wide
Were found, with rocks o'er-written by a pen,
Whose marks were yet a marvel and unread.
And Science breathed on men, and bade them scan
Whate'er was new and wonderful and strange.
Mountains were climbed ; and where volcanic fires
Poured forth their burning floods, and flashed
        their flames
In lurid grandeur 'gainst the starlit sky,
There Science took his way with studious step
To study Nature's Book of Mysteries.
He sought the leafy grove, the flow'ry plain,
The trickling rill, the fountain's cooling flow,
And Ocean's vast and yet defiant plain,
To learn of them their wonders.   These, when
        learned,
In dreams were whispered into human ears,
Till men, from deepest sleep, would start, surprised
At revelations which came, as the winds,
Whose source they knew not.   Phantom forms of
        things—

The air-drawn antitypes which were to be
The workman's guide to frame inventions* strange,
Would start from naught and seem reality.
And Art, through human hands would give them
      shape,
Moulding the wood, the metal and the clay,
As willing aids in man's progressive path.

  Time circles on : The storm-defying bark
Floats proudly o'er the waters : On the heights
The pride-suggested tower is upreared,
To penetrate above the fleecy clouds,
And solve the azure mysteries of heaven.
The brush, the pencil and the chisel seem
To glow with mystic life.   Beneath their touch
Dull matter put on an attractive guise
Of counterfeit existence.   These proclaim
The works of Art—of daring, skillful Art—
Who, when the earth was young in centuries,
Outstripped his god-like brother in the race,
And on his brow the boasted laurel bore.
Science approval gave ; his soaring thought,
Unenvious, traced the circuit of the stars ;
Read with deep skill the wondrous lore of heaven ;
Sought in the thunder-cloud its sacred fire,
And tamed it for man's use in after years ;
Stooped to the boiling caldron and inquired
Of steam its hidden force ; asked of the brook,
That laughed and danced along its pebbly way,

    * This term is used in a strictly mechanical sense.

If pow'r it had to turn the pond'rous wheel,
And, tireless, work ungrudgingly for man?
The answers were earth's riches. Long, long years
Careered through changeful seasons, and were lost
In the oblivious Lethe of the Past,
Ere the full force of all those mysteries
Could be impressed upon the finite mind.
Thus, in their relative though separate spheres,
Toiled Art and Science for the human race.
What Science pointed with prophetic thought
Art would embody with realities ;
And when Art failed in strivings for mankind,
Science suggested ready remedies.
The trembling needle, faithful to the pole,
Approves their joint endeavor. O'er the sea,
Through storm and darkness, still it points the
          way—
A trusted sentinel, which knows no change,
Though all around it changes. Theirs the skill
Which marries music to "immortal verse"
To chant progression's peans. Theirs the pow'r
Which chains the restive vapor to the car
And strong-bound bark, and bids it urge them on,
Fleet as the wind, though gravitation's laws
And fiercest storms opposing may defy.
Theirs is the might, whose god-light majesty
Has bound the electric messenger of heaven—
Made it the minister of human thought—
Taught it the varied languages of earth—
And sends it, swift as coursers of the sun,

O'er mountain tops—through seas—till distant
      lands
Whisper familiar in each other's ears,
As lovers, when together.   Vast and grand
As such twin triumphs are, they're still as naught,
Compared with wonders which are yet to be,
When Art and Science ope their ampler store !

ELLA LEE.

L IKE the stars which sparkle
      In the azure height,
Brightening the darkness,
   Beautifying night,
Are thine eyes to me,
Lovely Ella Lee—
Are thine eyes to me,
Oh, my lovely Ella Lee.

Like the rose which blushes
   In the garden fair,
Making purer, sweeter,
   All that's blooming there,
Are thy cheeks to me,
Lovely Ella Lee—
Are thy cheeks to me,
Oh, my lovely Ella Lee.

Like the rays of gladness,
   Early morning throws
Over fields and flowers,
   Blushing in repose,

Are thy smiles to me,
Lovely Ella Lee—
Are the smiles to me,
Oh, my lovely Ella Lee.

Like the ruby portals
  To the realms of bliss,
Where Elysian maidens
  Welcome with a kiss,
Are thy lips to me,
Lovely Ella Lee—
Are thy lips to me,
Oh, my lovely Ella Lee.

THE VOYAGE OF LIFE.

'TIS a morn in Spring, and the perfumed air
    Seems freighted with treasures of answered
        prayer ;
From the groves and hills come a matin song,
Which the sylvan echoes in joy prolong,
As if to tempt from the bending skies,
Sweet angel voices with kind replies.

Before me runneth a wondrous stream,
Bearing all things on like a changeful dream ;
There are hopes and joys, there are cares and
        tears,
There are cherished trophies of by-gone years ;
There are vessels laden with pearls and gold,
With the jewels bought, with the jewels sold,
With wealth that can neither be sold nor bought,
With thoughts that can neither be tamed nor
        taught,
With willing hearts—like the fruitful vine
Which yields at the harvest its oil or wine—
With care and shame, with disease and sin—
All that man can lose—all that man can win !

The stream is Time, and its onward roll
Is to that bright realm—the eternal goal,
Which the eye of Faith can discern afar
By the light of an uncreated Star.*

Now I see a bark pushing out from shore,
At the prow is Hope, at the stern an oar ;
In the midst two children awake to play,
While the bright sun silvers their shining way ;
They're young immortals and "outward bound"—
May their keel ne'er touch on enchanted ground !
May they safely pass by the tempting isles
Which pleasure gilds with deceitful smiles !
When the storms arise and the tempests blow,
In whom to trust may they always know.

See, tired of play, on their mother's breast
Now, calm and trustful, they sink to rest !
The father urgeth the shallop on
While the sea is calm—ere the light hath gone.

A change : There's a book on a teacher's knee,
In which thoughts take form that the eye can see.
The teacher teacheth the growing child,
And points to the fountains that, undefiled,
Pour forth for the world their refreshing streams,
Where the light of Science and Learning gleams.

* The Star of Bethlehem.

The teacher teacheth of earth and sky—
How the mortal form must decay and die ;
How the light of Wisdom and warmth of Love
Must come from supernal realms above,
And how, unyielding to Death's control,
Forever liveth the human soul.

What a noble labor, if rightly done !
What harvest treasures there may be won
From the goodly soil where each chosen seed
Bears a precious thought or a precious deed.

Still on and on doth the vessel glide ;
Still on and on, through the yielding tide.
They're glowing landscapes it passes now ;
The sun is gilding the mountain's brow,
And stream, and meadow, and hill, and plain,
Are singing gaily : " *Not made in vain !*"
When nature thus on the young heart smiles,
And Hope is pointing to laughing isles,
Is it strange that some will be led astray
Into paths which promise a golden way—
That seeking pleasure, they gather woes,
And feel the thorn when they pluck the rose ?

I see the vessel—she still moves on—
But where are the father and mother gone ?
Where are the sister and teacher, too ?
They have disappeared from my searching view.

Perhaps they sleep in the ocean caves,
Or were laid to rest in some land of graves.
It matters not—they are gone, all gone,
But still the vessel careereth on.

What sound is that ? 'tis a lover's sigh ;
Like a breathing zephyr it passes by ;
Both joy and sadness are in its tone,
But the lover who breathes it is not *alone !*
" Father and mother the son shall leave ;
And unto his wife he shall kindly cleave."

The radiant sun in his golden march
Hath wandered high up in the heavenly arch ;
And when again I the bark behold,
A tale of love and of life is told.
I see a wife and a mother there ;
They ask a husband's and father's care,
A sword and a helmet are hanging near,
With a trusty shield and a trusty spear,
And the proud man saith : " I'm secure from harm
In my own brave heart—in my own strong arm."

Boast not, O man, in thy pride of strength,
For the stoutest oak shall decay at length ;
Thy years glide on like a tale that's told ;
With each fleeting breath thou art growing old !

A storm !—The sky is becoming dark ;
There's danger now for that poor, frail bark,

For the winds, like demons, are howling by,
And the lightnings burst from an angry sky.
Where now are thy boasted sword and spear?
Thy shield and helmet? What! dost thou fear?
Art thou not lord of this lower earth—
A king, by the vested rights of birth?
Stretch forth thy hand by thy royal will,
And say to the tempest : " Peace ! be still !"

Ah, weak, indeed, is the might of man,
When it wars 'gainst a heav'n-appointed plan ;
And his highest light e'er in science won
Is a glow-worm's ray to the burning sun !

The storm is over. With humbler mien,
Now seated his wife and his son between,
The husband speaks of the dangers past,
And points to the Ocean, unknown and vast,
Where Faith discerneth the starry isles,
And Welcome weareth eternal smiles.
Husband and father ! mother and wife !
These are the ties of this lower life ;
These are the links of a golden chain
Which wrong and sorrow, and sin and pain,
Cannot wholly tarnish—the links of love
Which bind on earth as in heaven above.

Old age comes on, and approaching night
Casts a sadd'ning shade over all things bright,
Save the rosy tinge of the glowing West,
Which seems the smile of some land more blest.

The son now stands by the father's side ;
From a page illumed, as they onward glide,
He reads of a prisoner by Death set free—
Of the life beyond—of the Yet-to-Be.

Bear up, brave heart ! it is almost o'er,
For near appeareth a welcome shore,
A pleasant land where the roses twine—
A land which floweth with milk and wine.
Though the chill of death steals o'er thee now,
A holy halo enwreathes thy brow ;
And, waiting above thee, an angel band
Wave the *oriflamme* of the Better Land ;
They beckon thy soul from its house of clay,
And wait to bear thee away—away.

The sun has set, and the night appears.
A widowed mother I see in tears ;
O'er a lifeless body she bends in prayer,
And saith, " Ere long I shall join him there !"
Her finger points to the homes on high,
In the tearless realms of the upper sky.

NEW YEAR DAY.—JAN. 1ST, 1863.

I.

A NOTHER year is ended, and the glare
    Of burning cities lights the lurid sky.
Another year of carnage !   Where, O, where
Is Heav'n's avenging hand ?   Great God, draw
  - nigh,
List to the widow's wail ; the orphan's cry ;
Give speedy answer to a people's prayer ;
Send forth Thy rainbow-promise from on high ;
Make Sorrow's children Thy supernal care ;—
Give, gracious Giver, give—for thou alone canst
    spare.

II.

Joy bells are sounding !   This is New Year's day,
Flags flutter gaily in the wanton breeze ;
Proud martial notes discourse across the way,
And victor shouts are heard on land and seas.
These are War's triumphs !   These—not only
    these,
But blood, and desolation, and distress,
And tales of terror, such as well might freeze
The currents of young life.   O, who can bless
The fearful might of war, or welcome its caress ?

III.

Time was when Commerce thronged our busy
    streets ;
When Labor toiled for the rewards of peace ;
When every sea was whitened with the fleets
That brought or bore away our golden fleece.
But with war's triumphs those of Commerce cease.
The bugle's note has drowned the hum of trade.
" Business suspended " means a sad decrease
Of all life's comforts.   How pure home joys fade
When men for vengeance have through blood
    to wade !

IV.

Come, gentle Peace, come back to us again ;
Come in thy old and well-beloved guise ;
Come with the glories of thy happy reign ;
Come with the laws which freemen ever prize ;
Come as an answer to a people's cries ;
Come with the power to shield and to restrain :—
Thy laws are love, thy counsels ever wise,
And though thou never canst restore the slain,
There's healing in thy voice—a balm for every pain.

V.

Sorrow has draped our garments with its weeds ;
May joy again its blessed brightness bring.
From gaping wounds our stricken country bleeds;
Let peace unending from the carnage spring.

New trees shall blossom and new birds shall sing
Above the cold graves of the buried Years ;
Then to the lessons of the past we'll cling,
Washing away our errors with our tears ;
Seeking the Faith which guides, the Hope sublime
    which cheers.

VI.

'Then MERRY NEW YEAR's to the people all,—
Though merriment is sadly out of place,
When o'er our land descends a bloody pall,
Shading the forms of stateliness and grace.
Look to the Future :—By Hope's day-star trace
A horoscope in lines of living light,
And, ere the Past its record can erase,
Another sun shall rise, so purely bright
That all the land shall say—*It is no longer night !*

A POETICAL BOUQUET OF THE UNITED STATES.

Alphabetically Arranged.

ALABAMA.

ALA—alas ! fair Alabama stands,
    A crownless queen amid her fertile lands ;
While her fond river murmurs, " Here we rest !" *
A barbed arrow rankles in her breast.

ARKANSAS.

Ark of a people's hope, brave Arkansas,
Thy fabled " tooth-pick" is no longer law ;
But thy strong arm and earnest might shall prove
A land's redemption and the shield of love.

CALIFORNIA.

Come, California, all thy wealth unfold :—
Those streams are wine; those rocks are virgin gold.
Prolific Nature in some partial hour
Bestowed on thee her fairest, richest dower.

* " Here we rest," is the signification of the Indian word
Alabama.

COLORADO.*

A maid among the mountains, fair and strong :
Hail, Colorado ! Unto thee belong
The soul that thrills ; the eye whose liquid fire
Can burn in hate or kindle soft desire.

CONNECTICUT.

Con me this riddle : Canst connect *I cut*
With making wooden nutmegs ? Aye. Then shut
Thy double-bladed knife, and let thy pride
Point to what Art has with thy name allied.

DELAWARE.

Speak out, fair State ! and make the dell aware
That thou, in all thy modest worth, art there.
Through thy calm courts soft echoes faintly swell,
Like memories which moan in ocean's shell.

FLORIDA.

Fair, florid, flowery, Florida appears.
Unending summer zones her glowing years,
While the fresh fountains of unfading youth
Flow from their depths to pledge her love and
truth.

* There seems to be some question whether Colorado is a
State or not, but that is not at all surprising. We have some
eccentric individuals among us who deny that Louisiana is a
State.

GEORGIA.

Gay, gallant, great ! let Georgia arise,
Earnest in effort and in action wise.
Her fields are rich with nature's choicest stores,
And all her hills are veined with golden ores.

ILLINOIS.

O'er thy broad prairies peace and plenty reign ;
And milk and honey, golden fields of grain,
And flocks and herds are thine, proud Illinois :—
God make thee great, and crown thy homes with
   joy !

INDIANA.

If in Diana, of Ephesian fame,
Were "truth and honor," worthy of the name,
What words of praise can tell in fitting guise
Of Indiana, great and fair and wise ?

IOWA.

Proud Iowa, thy children's love of thee
Is kin to that which Venice gave the sea.
In minds, in lands, in men, in love, in hate ;
Thou peerless must appear—great 'mong the great !

KANSAS.

Cradled in strife ; bleeding at every vein ;
The stars looked down upon thee in thy pain,
And heav'n decreed that thy fresh blood should be
Cemented in the seal of Liberty.

KENTUCKY.

Brave are thy sons, thy daughters pure and
bright,
O, loyal land of liberty and light !
The laurel and the cypress both are thine,
And e'en thy Boone and " Bourbon " are divine.

LOUISIANA.

" Sweets to the sweet !"   Let Louisiana rise
And claim from rival hands proud beauty's
prize :
Fair as a Seraph's dream ; e'en through her tears
She shows the trust that wins, the smile that
cheers.

MARYLAND.

From the dark bosom of Potomac's wave
A wail comes forth, as voices from a grave :
Weep, Maryland bereav'd : for tears like thine
Cleanse like the flow of sacrificial wine.

MAINE.

Timber and tonnage ; sailors and the sea ;
Lakes, rivers, mountains—these belong to thee :
Work to thy sons is worship—conquest—gain—
For wise men are those " Maniacs " of Maine.

MASSACHUSETTS.

Now by the mass, old Massachusetts stands,
"Hub" and exampler to all other lands.
Strong in her faith, her learning and her might,
She kindles quarrels and bids others "fight !"

MICHIGAN.

The wooing waters claim thee as their bride ;
Round thy bold shores the gallant navies glide ;
And flood and field, rejoicing in thy fame,
Become the heralds of an honored name.

MINNESOTA.

Pride of the great Northwest ! In hill and dale,
In flocks and herds, in streams which never fail,
In grand old forests—thou hast wealth untold,
With health and freedom, dearer far than gold !

MISSISSIPPI.

Gallant in war, a conqueror in peace :
Thy flossy staple, more than "golden fleece,"
Brings riches to the world. No brighter sun
Than thine e'er beamed on glories to be won.

MISSOURI.

"Fixed as the centre." Throned o'er giant streams
Which course a continent. What mighty themes
Before thy seers and statists proudly rise,
Wooing thee on to deeds of high emprise.

NEBRASKA.*

Where rocky mountains, spined against the sky,
The thunder's rage and lightning's flash defy,
There, laved by restless rivers, thou art seen,
Making the wilds rejoice, the deserts green !

NEVADA.

Land of the snowy peaks and flowing streams :
No fabled Plutus mocks thee in thy dreams,
For all thy hills with argent wealth abound,
And e'en thy echoes have a silv'ry sound.

NORTH CAROLINA.

The *miserere* moans among thy pines,
While tears of amber flow.   These are the signs
Alike of thy great wealth and deep distress :—
Pine not,† proud State, but onward, upward
    press !

NEW HAMPSHIRE.

New Hampshire, hail ! fixed on thy granite base
There's stern defiance in thy rugged face.
Thy children smite the rock and they are fed ;
Thy ice is more than wine, thy stones than bread ?

* Though Nebraska has not yet been fully admitted into
the family of States, "an enabling act" has been passed in
her case, and she cannot be "kept out in the cold" much
longer.

† The printer's devil insisted, in this instance, that "not"
should be printed "knot." We, however, resisted him, and
sent the k off kiting.

NEW JERSEY.

O, Commonwealth supreme ! In sov'reign might,
Thou standest proudly in the nation's sight :
" Fair play," thy motto ; thy abhorrence, debt ;
Thy cherish'd self thou never canst forget.

NEW YORK.

Imperial State ! From Erie to the sea
Thy arms are stretched ; thy sisters bow to thee.
Great in thy commerce ; great in wealth and fame :
A thousand echoes syllable thy name.

OHIO.

Thy beauteous river, in its liquid flow,
Still chants thy name, and calls on friend and foe
To join in the great anthem of thy praise,
And bind around thy brow the poet's bays.

OREGON.

Where roll'd the Oregon and not "a sound
Save its own dashing," stirred the deep profound,
Now busy life and smiling fields appear,
And golden harvests crown the gladsome year.

PENNSYLVANIA.

Land of the peaceful Penn ! thy fruitful soil
Spreads o'er rich beds of coal and streams of oil ;
The Union's keystone and thy people's pride ;
Greater thy Penn than sword and spear allied !

RHODE ISLAND.

Bijou of States ! 'Tis said thy soldier sons
Must seck out larger lands to try their guns.
Isled in thy great success thou stand'st alone,
For skill and thrift have claimed thee as their own.

SOUTH CAROLINA.

Haughty and proud, the seared "Palmetto"
      stands,
Mantled with "Southern Rights." The high
      commands
Of her dead statesman claim obedience yet :
What she once learns she never can forget.

TENNESSEE.

Tender and true ! I greet thee, Tennessee !
Thy sorrow makes thee sacred. Who shall be
The bard to sing thy epic ? Words of fire,
To tell thy wrongs, should flash along his lyre !

TEXAS.

Land of broad meadows, corn, and oil, and
      wine—
Land of the neighing steed and grazing kine—
Land of fruit, flowers and ores—on man below,
No fairer heritage could heaven bestow.

VERMONT.

Crowned with their coronal of living green,
Thy mountain heights smile on the vales between ;
Fair, happy vales, where love and freedom reign,
Though winter storms should whiten all the plain.

VIRGINIA.

Mother of States and statesmen.   Heroes tread
Through thy historic halls.   Around thy head
A glory grandly circles.   Hail to thee !
Great in thy past—great shall thy future be !

WEST VIRGINIA.

O Child, dissevered from a noble line,
In thy new temple dost not sometimes pine
For the old hearth—the dear familiar ties—
Which, at the thought of home, should ever rise ?

WISCONSIN.

Thy woods and prairies in their summer pride
Have all the grace and beauty of a bride.
Brave in thy sons and fruitful in thy soil,
Thine are the triumphs of successful toil.

TIMES OFFICE, *New Orleans*, 1866.

TO-DAY.

FROM the tomb where buried ages
  Slumber on in calm repose,
Come the voices of the sages,
  Freed from all their weight of woes.
Theirs are no sad words of warning ;
  To our ears they seem to say :
" Hail the dawn !—another morning
  Ushers in a brighter day !"

Hail the dawn ! A glory rises
  From the brow of bard and seer :
Still the world is full of prizes ;
  Life is still a thing most dear :—
Let it not be clogged and fettered
  By dead chronicles and creeds ;
Waiting souls are only bettered
  By high thoughts and noble deeds.

But high thoughts and deeds to measure,
  Lower standards we must know ;
Fondest, keenest thrills of pleasure
  Are akin to pain and woe ;

Tears of joy and tears of sorrow
　From the self same liquid eyes
Flow at will ; then who would borrow
　Trouble from o'erclouded skies ?

What though from the tree of knowledge
　Bitter fruit may sometimes fall,
Where's the teacher in his college
　Who can promise good to all ?
Good and evil grow together ;
　Vice is only virtue's foil ;
Stormy winds in wintry weather
　Do not summer glories spoil.

Let us, then, with march progressive,
　Bravely. t'wards the goal advance ;
Worthy toil is not oppressive :
　Raise the banner ! poise the lance !
All around, the pregnant present
　Calls us from our childish play;
Teacher, thinker, peer and peasant,
　Aid us in our work to-day !

COMPENSATION.

THE earth is lying, green and fair, beneath
    God's eternal smile,
  But cries discordant pulse along the air from
    hill and wold ;
And who are these, the struggling hosts, that
    would our shrines defile,
  And sell the birthright of the free for merest
    dross of gold ?

These elder brothers are :—they claim a right
    divine to rule ;
  On covenants of selfishness they set the seal of
    blood ;
Unthinking swords and bayonets are teachers in
    their school ;
  Their argosies of privilege float o'er a purple
    flood.

Might makes *their* right. All who oppose are
    traitors and accurs'd,
  And all who meekly wear the yoke are " loyal
    men and true."

With bold presumption they would have all nature's laws revers'd,
And make the many everywhere the vassals of
the few.

"Seek out the weak: let them be taxed, while
we—the strong—divide
The honors and the profits, which are our un-
doubted right."
Such are the words of arrogance with which, in
heartless pride,
They issue cruel edicts and in selfishness unite.

But still the world moves grandly on, and Time,
the tester, tries
Whate'er is built on high resolves—whate'er is
mean and low—
He separates with potent art, the foolish from the
wise,
And gives to Truth his crown of light, to error
only woe.

The petty triumphs of to-day may be to-morrow's
ban ;
The failures which we so lament may prove a
source of joy.
Man's wisdom is but foolishness.   In Heaven's appointed plan
Life's mystic problem we evolve—we build and
we destroy.

What though contending millions meet in battle
    on the plain,
    And fiercely fight, and fiercely hate, and pite-
        ously bleed ?
The false cannot be made the true by hecatombs
    of slain,
    Nor can successes sanctify a base, ignoble deed.

Though all to human eyes seem dark, Jehovah
    rules unseen,
    And what appears as wrong and hate, may
        prove but notes of praise,
Soon as we reach the blissful fields of never-fading
    green,
Where floods of uncreated light illume earth's
    darksome ways.

TIMES OFFICE, *June*, 1866.

LINES.

[On receiving a pair of eye-glasses from a friend.]

NOW by my beard, this is a goodly sight !
   Transparent crystals set in frames of gold:
Through them, untaxed, the soft translucent light
   Comes to our eyes.   A miracle !   Behold—
The dim, dull, clouded page grows clear and bold,
   Thought's mystic foot-prints gleam forth full and
      bright,
As when the jewels in the robe of Night
   To the rapt gaze of Sibyl are unrolled.

NEW ORLEANS, *October*, 1865.

www.ingramcontent.com/pod-product-compliance
Lightning Source LLC
Chambersburg PA
CBHW020850270326
41928CB00006B/640